بسم الله الرحمن الرحيم

Allah's name I begin with,
the utmost Kind and ever Merciful

إن هذا القرآن يهدي للتي هي أقوم

"Indeed, this Qur'an guides to that which is most suitable"
(Surah Al-Isra', verse 9)

Name of Student: ______________________________

Name of Teacher: ______________________________

Date Started: ______________________________

Date Finished: ______________________________

المقدمة الجزرية

فى علم التجويد

لامام القراء شيخ الاسلام و المسلمين و خاتمة الحفاظ و المحدثين

أَبِي الْخَيرِ شَمْسِ الدِّيْنِ مُحَمَّدِ بْنِ مُحَمَّدِ بْنِ مُحَمَّدِ الْجَزَرِيِّ الدِّمَشْقِيِّ

رَحِمَهُ اللّٰهُ تَعَالٰى

(توفي 833 هـ)

شرحه ابو احمد فضل الحق

A brief commentary on

Muqaddimah Jazariyyah

Of Shaykh ul Islam Imam ibn Jazari

By the father of
Ahmad M Fazlehaq

Zein Hud Publications
Reviving the Classics

First Edition 2019

Published by
Zein Hud Publications
Birmingham
United Kingdom

zein.hud.publications@gmail.com

ISBN 978-1-9998185-3-1

Zein Hud Publications
Reviving the Classics

Printed by Mega Printing in Turkey

Contents

Ijazah in the Poem.. 6
Introduction to *Imam Ibn Jazari*.................................. 7
Touching and reciting the *Qur'an* 8
The Rhythmic Scale of The Poem.................................. 10
The Introduction.. 13
Makharij – Points of Articulation................................ 19
Sifaat – Attributes of Letters...................................... 37
Tajweed.. 51
Tafkhim, *Tarqiq* and Some Important Points.................. 57
The Letter *Ra*.. 65
The Letter *Laam* and Various Rules............................... 69
Idgham of *Mutamaathilayn* and *Mutajaanisayn*............... 75
The Letter *Dhad* and *Zha*.. 79
Advices... 89
Nun and *Mim Mushaddadatayn* and *Mim Sakinah*........ 91
Nun Sakinah and *Tanween*.. 95
Madd.. 99
Knowing Where to Stop and Start.................................. 103
Detached and Attached Words..................................... 111
Ta.. 125
Hamzat ul-Wasl... 131
Waqf... 135
The Ending... 139
Test 141

الاجازة في المَنْظُومَةِ الْجَزَرِيَّةِ

اَلْحَمْدُ للهِ الَّذِيْ أَنْزَلَ الْقُرْآنَ مُرَتَّلًا تَرْتِيْلًا وَ وَعَدَ مَنْ قَرَأَه وَ عَمِلَ بِه ثَوَابًا جَزِيْلًا وَ الصَّلَاةُ و السَّلَامُ عَلى أَفْصَحِ مَنْ نَطَقَ بِالضَّادِ سَيِّدِنَا مُحَمَّدٍ وَ عَلى آلِه وَ أَصْحَابِه وَ مَنْ تَبِعَهُمْ بِإِحْسَانٍ إلى يَوْمِ الدِّيْنِ

أَمَّا بَعْدُ فَيَقُولُ العَبْدُ الضَّعِيْفُ الفقيْرُ الى رَبِّه القَوِيّ الغَنِيّ زَين هود بن محمد اخلاق الازهري فقد أَجَازَنِيْ الشيخ أشرف حامد حسانين في المَنْظُومَةِ الْجَزَرِيَّةِ و هو قَرَأَهَا على الشيخ العلامة عَبدِ الفتَّاح بن مدكور بن بيومي و هو على العلامة المدقق علي محمد الضباع وهو على الشيخ عبد الرحمن الخطيب الشعار وهو على الشيخ محمد أحمد المتولى و هو على الشيخ أحمد الدري التهامي و هو على الشيخ أحمد بن محمد المعروف بسلمونة وهو على الشيخ إبراهيم العبيدي الازهري المالكي و هو على الشيخ عبد الرحمن الأجهوري و هو على الشيخ أحمد البقري و هو على الشيخ محمد البقري وهو على الشيخ عبد الرحمن شحاذة اليمنى و هو على الشيخ على بن محمد المقدسي وهو على الشيخ السمديسي وهو على الشيخ أحمد بن أسد الأميوطي و هو على الامام المحقق المدقق المقرئ المعروف بابن الجزري رحمهم الله تعالى .

هذا وَ إني قد أجزتُ خَادم / خَادِمة القرآن و العلم

بعد أن قرأ / قَرَأَتْ عليَّ المَنْظومَةَ الجَزَرِيَّةَ لِشَيْخِ الاسلام ابن الجزري رحمه الله تعالى بجمبعِ مَا يجوز لي رِوَايتُه و صَحَّ عَني درايتُه إجازةً صَحيحةً بشرطها المعتبر عند اهل الحديث و الأثر و له أن يَرْوِيَهَا عَنِّي و يُجِيْزَ غَيْرَه بِهَا وَأسأل الله العظيم ان يزيده من فضله علما وايمانا وصلى الله على سيدنا محمد وآله وصحبه وسلم والحمد لله رب العالمين.

المجيز

الفقير الى الله تعالى

زين هود بن محمد أخلاق الازهري

مدرس القرآن و العلوم الشرعية بدار القراء و مركز البحوث الاسلامية

التوقيع: التاريخ:

IMAM IBN JAZARI

لامام القراء شيخ الاسلام و المسلمين

أَبُو الْخَيرِ شَمْسُ الدِّيْنِ مُحَمَّدُ بْنِ مُحَمَّدِ بْنِ مُحَمَّدِ الْجَزَرِيّ الدِّمَشْقِيّ

رَحِمَهُ اللهُ تَعَالَى

Imam ibn Jazari ﷺ was born in Damascus in the year 751 A.H on the 25 of *Ramadhan*. He memorised the *Qur'an* by the age of 13 and studied the sciences of the *Qur'an* and *Fiqh*. After completing his studies in Damascus, he travelled to Egypt to advance his knowledge in *Fiqh*, *Hadith*, *Usul*, *Balaghah* and many other sciences. His knowledge of *Qira'ah* was incomparable, which led him to travel extensively throughout the Islamic world teaching the science of *Qira'ah* and *Tajweed*. He passed away on Friday 5 *Rabi' ul Awwal* year 833 A.H in *Shiraz*.

Some of his famous works:

النَّشْرُ فِي القِرَاءَاتِ الْعَشْرِ

تَقْرِيْبُ النَّشْرِ فِي القِرَاءَاتِ الْعَشْرِ (هو مختصر لكتابه النشر في القِرَاءَاتِ الْعَشْرِ)

طَيْبَةُ النَّشْرِ فِي القِرَاءَاتِ الْعَشْرِ (منظومة على نهج كتابه النشر في القِرَاءَاتِ الْعَشْرِ)

غَايَةُ النِّهَايَةِ فِي طَبَقَاتِ الْقُرَّاءِ

اَلْمُقَدِّمَةُ الْجَزَرِيَّةُ

التَمْهِيْدُ فِي عِلْمِ التَّجْوِيْدِ

And many more

TOUCHING AND RECITING THE QUR'AN

After a careful study of the *Qur'an* and *Sunnah*, Muslim jurists have mentioned that purity is a condition to touch the *Qur'an*. For example, Allah ﷻ states in the *Qur'an*:

لَّا يَمَسُّهُۥٓ إِلَّا ٱلْمُطَهَّرُونَ

"Do not touch it except those that are pure"

(*Surah al-Waqi'ah* verse 79)

Furthermore, there are many *Ahadith* that mention purity as a condition, for example *Abdullah ibn Abi Bakr ibn Hazm* ؓ narrates:

أَنَّ فِي الْكِتَابِ الَّذِي كَتَبَهُ رَسُولُ اللَّهِ صلى الله عليه وسلم لِعَمْرِو بْنِ حَزْمٍ أَنْ لَّا يَمَسَّ الْقُرْآنَ إِلاَّ طَاهِرٌ

"*In the letter, which the Messenger of Allah* ﷺ *wrote to 'Amr ibn Hazm, it states that no one should touch the Qur'an, except those that are pure.*"

(*al-Mu'atta of Imam Malik*)

MAJOR IMPURITY AND MENSES

Reciting of by heart

In the state of menses and major impurity, which necessitates a full bath, reciting the *Qur'an* in prohibited, even of by heart. However, sending salutations, supplicating in Arabic or reciting other *Awrad* is permissible, even if they contain some phrases from the *Qur'an*, as the intension is not to recite the *Qur'an* but rather to remember Allah ﷻ or to supplicate. In such situations, it is desirable to perform ablution prior to supplicating or reciting the *Awrad*.

On the other hand, scholars have mentioned that it is permissible to recite the *Qur'an* by thought and not the tongue. Therefore, thinking and contemplating over the words of the *Qur'an* is permissible.

Touching the *Qur'an*

It is permissible to look at the *Qur'an* in the state of major impurity or menses, but not to touch it. It is not permissible to touch the *Qur'an* when a person is impure, even if it is a blank page in the *Qur'an* that has no writing on it.

MINOR IMPURITY – NOT HAVING ABLUTION

Reciting of by heart

It is permissible to recite the *Qur'an* of by heart without touching it physically, whilst not having ablution.

Touching the Qur'an

Touching the *Qur'an* without ablution is not permissible, unless it is via a glove or other barrier, so long as it is not something attached to the *Qur'an*. If a cover has been attached to the *Qur'an*, then touching that is also not permissible. The barrier needs to be something separate, like a clean piece of cloth or a wooden stick.

If a paper or book contains some verses of the *Qur'an*, it is not permissible to touch the actual verse of the *Qur'an* without ablution. However, touching other parts of that paper or book is permissible, although it is preferable to have ablution.

THE RHYTHMIC SCALE OF THE POEM

Arabic poems are written on rhythmic patterns, known as *Buhur*, (بُحُوْر) which is the plural of *Bahr*. The science that studies the rhythmic patterns of poems is called *'Ilm ul- 'Arudh* (علم العروض). Although, these rhythmic patterns were used in pre-Islamic poetry, as a science it was developed by famous grammarian of the Arabic language, *Imam Al-Khaleel bin Ahmad Al-Faraheedi.*

This poem has been written on the rhythmic pattern known as *Bahr ur-Rajaz* (بَحْرُ الرَّجَز) that falls on the scale of مُسْتَفْعِلُنْ which appears six times in a verse. A word will fall on this rhythmic scale if it's vowelized and *Sakin* letters match the scale *Mustaf'ilun*. For example:

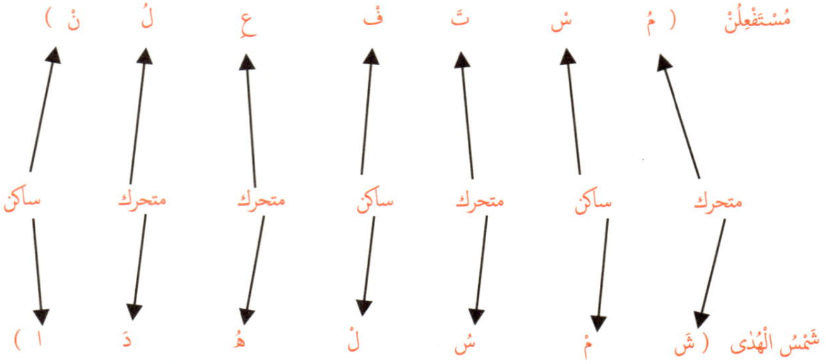

The pattern can also be illustrated using the symbol (/) for a *Mutaharrik* letter and the letter (o) for a *Sakin* letter, in the following way:

مُسْتَفْعِلُنْ (o / / o / o /)

SOME TERMINOLOGY

A couplet is called *Bayt* (بيت). It is made up of two parts, the first is called *Sadr* (صَدْر) and the second is called *'Ajuz* (عَجُز).

البيت = مُسْتَفْعِلُنْ مُسْتَفْعِلُنْ مُسْتَفْعِلُنْ . . . مُسْتَفْعِلُنْ مُسْتَعِلُنْ مُسْتَفْعِلُنْ

صَدْر   عَجُز

A scale is called *Taf'ilah* (تَفْعِيْلَة) and the last scale in the *Sadr* is called *'Arudh* (عَرُوض), whilst the last scale in the *'Ajuz* is called *Darb* (ضَرْب).

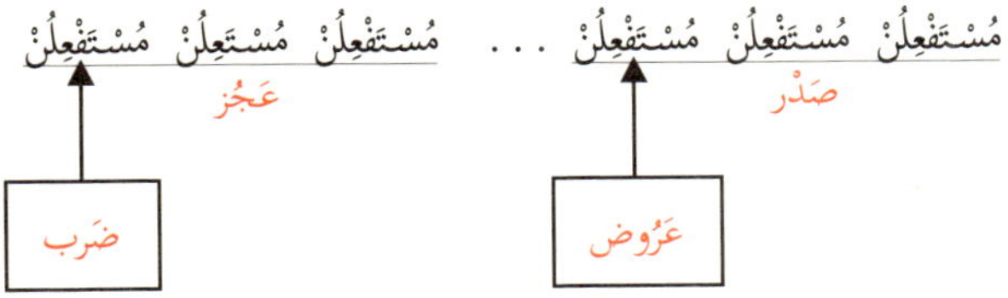

ZIHAAF (زِحَاف)

This scale has three other variations, which are created by removing the *Sakin* letters from the scale. The three scales are:

1. مُتَفْعِلُنْ (o//o//): The first *Sakin* letter (س) has been removed to create this new scale. This change is called *Khabn* (خبن).
2. مُسْتَعِلُنْ (o///o/): The second *Sakin* letter (ف) has been removed. This change is called *Tay* (طَي).
3. مُتَعِلُنْ (o////): The first two *Sakin* letters have been removed. This change is called *Khabl* (خَبل).

Note: Sometimes in the *Darb* (ضَرب) the last *Sakin* letter (ن) is removed from the scale and the *Laam* is made *Sakin:* مُسْتَفْعِلْ (o/o/o/). This is called *Qat'* (قَطْع).

ANALYSIS OF THE FIRST VERSE IN THIS POEM

There are three essential steps to testing the rhythmic pattern of a poem:

1. All *Mushaddad* letters must be written without *Idgham*.
2. Every *Tanween* must be written as a *Nun Sakin*.
3. The letters that are not pronounced are taken out.

In short, rewrite the line according to how its pronounced.

Original verse:

يَقُولُ رَاجِي عَفْوِ رَبٍّ سَامِعِ ... مُحَمَّدُ بْنُ الْجَزَرِيِّ الشَّافِعِي

After the steps:

يَقُولُ رَاجِي عَفْوِ رَبْبِنْ سَامِعِي ... مُحَمْمَدُ بْنُ لْجَزَرِيْيِ شْشَافِعِيْ

o//o/o/ o///o/ o//o// . . . o//o/o/ o//o/o/ o//o//

مُتَفْعِلُنْ مُسْتَفْعِلُنْ مُسْتَفْعِلُنْ . . . مُتَفْعِلُنْ مُسْتَعِلُنْ مُسْتَفْعِلُنْ

The books that I relied on when writing this brief commentary:

1. النشر في القراءات العشر لشيخ الاسلام بن الجزري الشافعي (ت 833 هـ)
2. المِنَحُ الْفِكْرِيَّةُ شرح المقدمة الجزرية لملا على بن سلطان محمد القاري الحنفي (ت 1014 هـ)
3. الدقائق الْمُحْكَمَةُ في شرح المقدمة لشيخ الاسلام زكريا الانصاري الشافعي (ت 936 هـ)
4. الفَوَائدُ المسعديّة في حل الجزرية للامام عمر بن ابراهيم بن علي المسعدي (ت 1017 هـ)
5. الفوائد المفهمة في شرح الجزرية المقدمة لابي عبد الله فخر الدين محمد بن علي بن يوسف بن يالوشه التونسي المالكي (ت 1314 هـ)
6. الطرازاتُ المعلمة في شرح المقدمة لشيخ عبد الدائم الازهري (ت 870 هـ)
7. الفوائد الجلية شرح المقدمة الجزرية لمحمود رأفت بن حسن زلط
8. الروضة الندية شرح متن الجزرية لمحمود بن محمد بن عبد المنعم العبد

بسم الله الرحمن الرحيم

المقدمة

The Introduction

[1] يَقُولُ رَاجِي عَفْوِ رَبٍّ سَامِعِ ... مُحَمَّدُ بْنُ الْجَزَرِيِّ الشَّافِعِي

[2] الْحَمْدُ لِلهِ وَصَلَّى اللهُ ... عَلَى نَبِيِّهِ وَمُصْطَفَاهُ

[3] مُحَمَّدٍ وَآلِهِ وَصَحْبِهِ ... وَمُقْرِئِ الْقُرْآنِ مَعْ مُحِبِّهِ

[4] وَبَعْدُ إِنَّ هَذِهِ مُقَدِّمَهْ ... فِيمَا عَلَى قَارِئِهِ أَنْ يَعْلَمَهْ

[5] إِذْ وَاجِبٌ عَلَيْهِمُ مُحَتَّمُ ... قَبْلَ الشُّرُوعِ أَوَّلًا أَنْ يَعْلَمُوا

[6] مَخَارِجَ الْحُرُوفِ وَالصِّفَاتِ ... لِيَلْفِظُوا بِأَفْصَحِ اللُّغَاتِ

[7] مُحَرِّرِي التَّجْوِيدِ وَالْمَوَاقِفِ ... وَمَا الَّذِي رُسِّمَ فِي الْمَصَاحِفِ

[8] مِنْ كُلِّ مَقْطُوعٍ وَمَوْصُولٍ بِهَا ... وَتَاءِ أُنْثَى لَمْ تَكُنْ تُكْتَبْ بِهَا

Note: The endings of the couplets that have the vowel (ُ) should be read with *Ishba'*, for example, مُحَتَّمُ should be read as مُحَتَّمُو. Likewise, the words that do not have an ending vowel, should be read with a *Karsah* as well as *Ishba'*. For example, اللُّغَات should be pronounced as اللُّغَاتِي

Imam Ibn al-Jazari ﷰ opens his poem by praising Allah ﷻ and sending *Salawat* upon his beloved messenger ﷺ :

[1] يَقُولُ رَاجِي عَفْوِ رَبٍّ سَامِعِ ... مُحَمَّدُ بْنُ الْجَزَرِيِّ الشَّافِعِي

Says, the seeker of forgiveness from the all hearing Lord,
Muhammad the son of Al-Jazari ash-Shafi'i

[2] الْحَمْدُ للهِ وَصَلَّى اللهُ ... عَلٰى نَبِيِّهِ وَمُصْطَفَاهُ

All praise is for Allah and peace and blessings of Allah
Be upon his Prophet, his chosen one

[3] مُحَمَّدٍ وَآلِهِ وَصَحْبِهِ ... وَمُقْرِئِ الْقُرْآنِ مَعْ مُحِبِّهِ

Muhammad, his family and his companions
And the reciter of Qur'an with its lover

[4] وَبَعْدُ إِنَّ هَذِهِ مُقَدِّمَهْ ... فِيمَا عَلَى قَارِئِهِ أَنْ يَعْلَمَهْ

And after, this is a primer
In that which is necessary upon the reciter to know

[5] إِذْ وَاجِبٌ عَلَيْهِمُ مُحَتَّمُ ... قَبْلَ الشُّرُوعِ أَوَّلًا أَن يَّعْلَمُوا

As it is indispensable upon them, certainly,
Before beginning to first know...

[6] مَخَارِجَ الْحُرُوفِ وَالصِّفَاتِ ... لِيَلْفِظُوا بِأَفْصَحِ اللُّغَاتِ

The points of articulation and characteristics (of letters)
So that they recite with the most eloquent of languages

[7] مُحَرِّرِي التَّجْوِيدِ وَالْمَوَاقِفِ ... وَمَا الَّذِي رُسِّمَ فِي الْمَصَاحِفِ

Whilst being experts in Tajweed and Waqf
And that which has been inscribed in the Masahif...

[8] مِنْ كُلِّ مَقْطُوعٍ وَمَوْصُولٍ بِهَا ... وَتَاءِ أُنْثَى لَمْ تَكُنْ تُكْتَبْ بِهَا

...from words that are detached and attached
And the feminine 'Ta', which is not written as a 'Ha'

The contents of the poem outlined in these couplets are:

1. *Makharij*
2. *Sifaat*
3. Places and method of stoppage
4. The *Uthmani* script concerning:
   a. Attached and detached words
   b. The letter '*Ta*' of feminine and its script

MAKHARIJ AND SIFAAT

Makharij is the plural of *Makhraj*, which refers to the point of articulation for a letter. In other words, the place where the letter is pronounced from. Whereas, *Sifaat* is the plural of *Sifah*, which refers to the attribute of a letter that specifies the quality of sound. Every letter will have a *Makhraj* and a set of *Sifaat*, both of which distinguish a letter from rest.

Compare the letter ج and ش . The *Makhraj* of both letters is the middle part of the tongue, known as *Wast ul-Lisaan*, yet both letters sound different. The difference in sound is a result of them differing in their *Sifaat*. For example, the flow of breath and sound stops in the letter *Jeem*, whilst in the letter *Sheen* the breath and sound continue to flow.

PLACES AND METHOD OF STOPPAGE

Knowing where to stop and how to stop correctly during recitation is very important, as stopping at an inappropriate place will change the meaning of a verse. For example:

أَلَمْ تَرَ إِلَى الَّذِي حَاجَّ إِبْرَاهِيمَ فِي رَبِّهِ أَنْ آتَاهُ اللَّهُ الْمُلْكَ إِذْ قَالَ إِبْرَاهِيمُ رَبِّيَ الَّذِي يُحْيِي وَيُمِيتُ
قَالَ أَنَا أُحْيِي وَأُمِيتُ ۖ قَالَ إِبْرَاهِيمُ فَإِنَّ اللَّهَ يَأْتِي بِالشَّمْسِ مِنَ الْمَشْرِقِ فَأْتِ بِهَا مِنَ الْمَغْرِبِ
فَبُهِتَ الَّذِي كَفَرَ ۗ وَاللَّهُ لَا يَهْدِي الْقَوْمَ الظَّالِمِينَ

"Do you not see the one who quarrelled with Ibrahim about his Lord, because Allah gave him Kingdom? When Ibrahim said: My Lord is He who gives life and causes death. He said: I give life and cause death. Ibrahim

said 'Well Allah brings the sun from the East; bring it from the West! Thereupon, became baffled the disbeliever. And Allah guides not the unjust people." (Surah Baqarah verse 258*)*

This verse mentions the challenge of *Nimrod* who is referred to as the disbeliever. In the last section of this verse, which is highlighted in red, if a person, instead of stopping at the words '*became baffled the disbeliever*' (فَبُهِتَ الَّذِىْ كَفَرَ), stopped after the words '*became baffled the disbeliever and Allah*' (فَبُهِتَ الَّذِىْ كَفَرَ ۗ وَاللّٰهُ), then the meaning of the verse will become extremely distorted, implying that the infidel and Allah, both, became baffled. If such distortion is done deliberately, a person will become a disbeliever.

Just like stopping at the wrong place will distort the meaning, likewise, not stopping at a compulsory stop will also distort the meaning. For example:

فَلَا يَحْزُنْكَ قَوْلُهُمْ ۘ اِنَّا نَعْلَمُ مَا يُسِرُّوْنَ وَمَا يُعْلِنُوْنَ

"*So, don't let their speech sadden you. We know what they conceal and what they announce.*"

When recited with a pause, the second part of this verse '*We know what they conceal and what they announce*' is correctly understood as the word of Allah ﷻ, in which 'We' indicates to Allah ﷻ, and 'they' indicates to the disbelievers. However, the absence of a stop would, incorrectly, give the impression that this is the speech of the disbelievers, which saddened the Prophet ﷺ. Hence, stopping and taking a breath in this verse is necessary.

UTHMANI SCRIPT

Knowledge of the script of the *Qur'an* as composed by the third Caliph, *Uthman* ؓ, is important. Every copy of the *Qur'an* available today has been written in the same script as the copies sent by *Uthman* ؓ to different Islamic cities, during his caliphate. Understanding the script, prior to recitation, is essential, as accurate pronunciation is not possible without knowing the script. The two essential aspects of the *Uthmani* Script, for the reciter to know, are concerning attached and detached words and the script for the *Ta* of feminine.

ATTACHED AND DETACHED WORDS

There are certain places in the *Uthmani* script, where two words have been combined in writing, whilst in other places the same two words are written detached. For example, the two words بِئْسَ and مَا are written detached in all places except in the following three verses:

بِئْسَمَا اشْتَرَوْا بِهٖٓ اَنْفُسَهُمْ (*Surah Baqarah* verse 90)

قَالَ بِئْسَمَا خَلَفْتُمُوْنِىْ مِنْۢ بَعْدِىْ (*Surah A'raaf* verse 150)

قُلْ بِئْسَمَا يَاْمُرُكُمْ بِهٖٓ اِيْمٰنُكُمْ اِنْ كُنْتُمْ مُّؤْمِنِيْنَ (*Surah Baqarah* verse 93)

However, in the last verse mentioned above, there is a difference of opinion concerning whether or not بِئْسَ and مَا in the *Uthmani* script are written attached or detached. Nonetheless, in every other place they are written separately. For example:

فَبِئْسَ مَا يَشْتَرُوْنَ (*Surah Aal-Imran*, verse 187)

THE LETTER *TA* OF FEMININE

At times the letter *Ta* of feminine has been written as a round *Ha* with dots, for example:

وَمَآ اَرْسَلْنٰكَ اِلَّا رَحْمَةً لِّلْعٰلَمِيْنَ

"*We have not sent you (O Muhammad) but as a mercy for all worlds.*"
(*Surah Al-Anbiya'*, verse 107)

The word mercy in Arabic is a feminine word, even though in meaning it is neither masculine nor feminine. The *Ta* at the end of this word is classified as a sign of feminine. In the above verse the *Ta* is written as a round *Ha* with dots, whilst in a few other places it is written as an open *Ta*, for example:

اِنَّ الَّذِيْنَ اٰمَنُوْا وَ الَّذِيْنَ هَاجَرُوْا وَجٰهَدُوْا فِيْ سَبِيْلِ اللّٰهِ ۙ اُولٰٓئِكَ يَرْجُوْنَ رَحْمَتَ اللّٰهِ ؕ وَاللّٰهُ
غَفُوْرٌ رَّحِيْمٌ

"Indeed, those have faith, migrate and struggle in the cause of Allah, they are the ones who desire the mercy of Allah, and Indeed Allah is forgiving and merciful."
(Surah Al-Baqarah, verse 217*)*

باب مخارج الحروف
Points of Articulation

[9] مَخَارِجُ الْحُرُوفِ سَبْعَةَ عَشَرْ ... عَلَى الَّذِي يَخْتَارُهُ مَنِ اخْتَبَرْ

[10] فَأَلِفُ الْجَوْفِ وَأُخْتَاهَا وَهِيْ ... حُرُوفُ مَدٍّ لِلْهَوَاءِ تَنْتَهِيْ

[11] ثُمَّ لِأَقْصَى الْحَلْقِ هَمْزٌ هَاءُ ... ثُمَّ لِوَسْطِهِ فَعَيْنٌ حَاءُ

[12] أَدْنَاهُ غَيْنٌ خَاؤُهَا و الْقَافُ ... أَقْصَى اللِّسَانِ فَوْقُ ثُمَّ الْكَافُ

[13] أَسْفَلُ وَالْوَسْطُ فَجِيمُ الشِّينُ يَا ... وَ الضَّادُ مِنْ حَافَتِه إِذْ وَلِيَا

[14] الَاضْرَاسَ مِنْ أَيْسَرَ أَوْ يُمْنَاهَا ... وَ اللَّامُ أَدْنَاهَا لِمُنْتَهَاهَا

[15] وَ النُّونُ مِنْ طَرَفِه تَحْتُ اجْعَلُوا ... وَ الرَّا يُدَانِيه لِظَهْرٍ أَدْخَلُ

[16] وَ الطَّاءُ وَ الدَّالُ وَ تَا مِنْهُ وَمِنْ ... عُلْيَا الثَّنَايَا وَ الصَّفِيرُ مُسْتَكِنْ

[17] مِنْهُ وَمِنْ فَوْقِ الثَّنَايَا السُّفْلَى ... وَ الظَّاءُ وَ الذَّالُ وَ ثَا لِلْعُلْيَا

[18] مِنْ طَرَفَيْهِمَا وَمِنْ بَطْنِ الشَّفَهْ ... فَالْفَا مَعَ اطْرَافِ الثَّنَايَا الْمُشْرِفَهْ

[19] لِلشَّفَتَيْنِ الْوَاوُ بَاءٌ مِّيْمٌ ... وَ غُنَّةٌ مَّخْرَجُهَا الْخَيْشُومُ

THE NUMBER OF ARABIC LETTERS

There are 29 letters in the Arabic alphabet according to all of the scholars of *Basrah*, except *Imam Mubarrad*. He classifies the *Alif* and *Hamzah* as one letter. His argument is that the name of every letter begins with that same letter, for example the name of the letter *Jeem* (جيم) begins with a *Jeem* (ج) and the name of the *Seen* (سين) begins with a *Seen* (س) and so forth. He applies this argument to the *Alif*, stating that the name *Alif* (ألِف) begins with a *Hamzah*, therefore the *Alif* and *Hamzah* are the same word.

In response to this argument, *Mulla Ali al-Qari* states in his commentary of *Jazariyyah*:

وَ أُجِيْبَ بِلُزُومِ أَنَّ الهمزةَ تَكونُ هَاءً لأَنَّهَا أولُ اسمِها

"*I respond that this [argument] will necessitate the Hamzah to be the same as a Ha, since its name begins with a Ha.*"

The difference between the *Hamzah* and the *Alif* is mentioned on the next page.

MAKHARIJ OF THE 29 LETTERS

There is a difference of opinion concerning the number of *Makharij* for the 29 letters. According to *Imam Sebaway* the *Makharij* are 16 in total, whilst *Imam Farra'* holds the opinion that there are 14 *Makharij*. However, according to most other scholars, there are 17 *Makharij* and this is the opinion advanced in this poem by *Imam ibn al-Jazari*.

[9] مَخَارِجُ الحُرُوفِ سَبْعَةَ عَشَرْ ... عَلَى الَّذِي يَخْتَارُهُ مَنِ اخْتَبَرْ

The points of articulation of letters are seventeen
[based] upon that which is the chosen [opinion] of those who research

The First *Makhraj* - *Al-Jawf* (The hollow space in the mouth and throat)

[10] فَ[مَخْرَجُ] أَلِف الجَوْفُ وَ [كذلك] أُخْتَاهَا وَهِي ... حُرُوفُ مَدٍّ لِلْهَوَاءِ تَنْتَهِي

The Alif is from the hollow mouth and [so are] its two sisters (Waw Maddah & Ya Maddah), and these...
...are the Madd letters, which end in the air

The *Jawf* is the *Makhraj* for the three *Madd* letters, which are:

Alif Maddah (Alif preceded by a Fathah)	قَالَ
Waw Maddah (Waw preceded by a Dhammah)	وَطُوْرِ
Ya Maddah (Ya preceded by a Kasrah)	سِيْنِيْنَ

Alif is a unique letter in the Arabic alphabet for the following two reasons, which are not found in any other letter:

a. It is always *Sakin*. However, if it seems that an *Alif* is vowelized, then that is a *Hamzah* and not an *Alif*. The *Hamzah* is commonly mistaken to be an *Alif*, because it is sometimes written like an *Alif*. In the following examples the letter in red ink is a *Hamzah* and not an *Alif*, because it is vowelised:

اَكْبَرُ - اِنَّ - اُمِّيُّوْنَ

There are two differences between a *Hamzah* and an *Alif*: First, A *Hamzah* can be vowelized but an *Alif* cannot, and second, when both are *Sakin*, the *Hamzah* has a sudden glottal stop, whereas the *Alif* has a smooth finish. Observe the difference in pronunciation of the following two examples:

قَالَ - بَأْسِ

b. The *Alif* is always preceded by a *Fathah*, which means it will always be a *Madd* letter and pronounced using the *Jawf.* Whilst other letters, including the *Hamzah* can be preceded by any vowel. Furthermore, this also differentiates *Alif Maddah* from the other two *Madd* letters, as *Waw* and *Ya* are not always *Madd* letters.

Note: it is important to remember that the *Waw* and *Ya* are only pronounced from the *Jawf*, when they are *Madd* letters, in any other state they have a different *Makhraj*, which will be mentioned later in this section.

The sound of all three *Madd* letters travels through the hollow space of the throat and mouth and eventually fades away in the air outside of the mouth. Whereas, in the other letters of the Arabic alphabet the sound does not seem to fade away into the air, but rather, it seems to be restricted by their *Makhraj.* To put this another way, the sound is restricted by the *Makhraj* using some part of the mouth or throat in every Arabic letter except the *Madd* letters, where the sound does not have any barrier. For this reason, the sound seems to fade away in the air rather than the mouth.

The next three *Makharij* are in the throat.

Second *Makhraj* – *Aqsal Halq* (The furthest part of the throat)

Aqsal Halq is that part of the throat where the vocal cords are located. The vocal cords sit above the wind pipe in the Larynx. This is the *Makhraj* of *Hamzah* (ء) and *Ha* (ه).

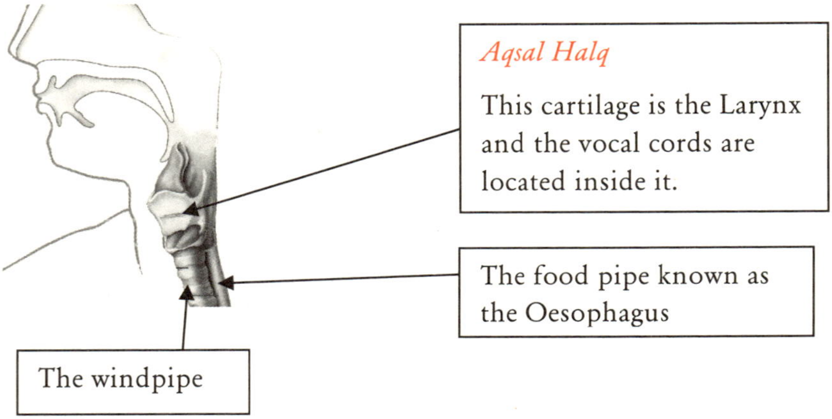

Third *Makhraj* – *Wastul Halq* (The middle part of the throat)

Wastul Halq is the flap near the root of the tongue and just above the Larynx, known as the Epiglottis. The function of it is to close the windpipe when food is swallowed to prevent it from entering the windpipe. When it closes the food is channelled down the food pipe, known as the Oesophagus.

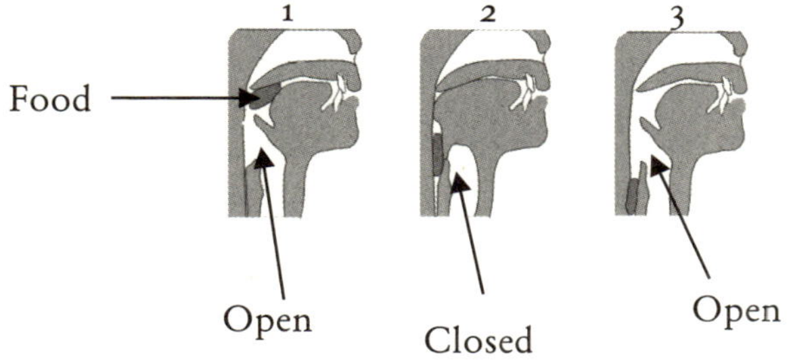

The Epiglottis can also be used to narrow the opening of the windpipe. This causes the air to flow out of a tight space, creating the sound of the letter *Ha* (ح). This is the *Makhraj* of *Ha* (ح) and *'Ayn* (ع).

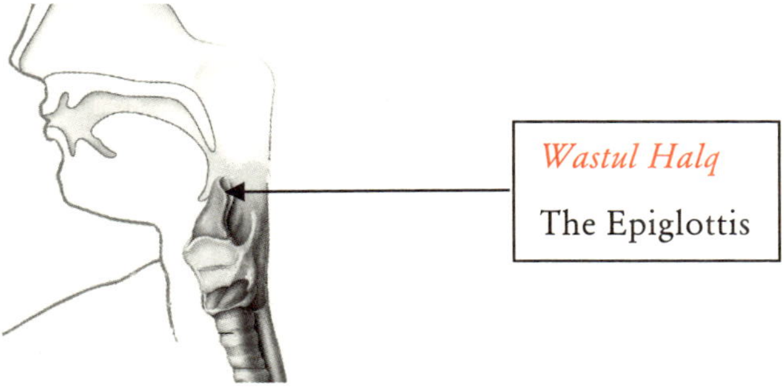

Forth *Makhraj* – *Adnal Halq* (The nearest part of the throat)

Adnal Halq is that part of the throat which is nearest to the mouth and just behind the Uvula. The root of the tongue and *Adnal Halq* are used together to pronounce *Ghayn* (غ) and *Kha* (خ).

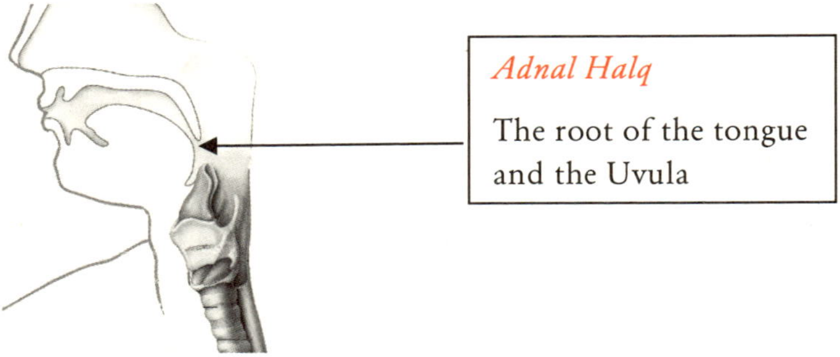

Imam ibn al-Jazari ﷺ mentions the three *Makharij* as follows:

[11] ثُمَّ لأَقْصَى الحَلْقِ هَمْزٌ هَاءُ ... ثُمَّ لِوَسْطِهِ فَعَيْنٌ حَاءُ

Then from the furthest part of the throat is Hamzah and Ha
And from its middle is 'Ain and Haa

[12] أَدْنَاهُ غَيْنٌ خَاؤُهَا ....

[from] its nearest part is Ghayn and its Kha.................…

As the next ten *Makharij* use the tongue and other parts of the inner mouth, it is important to learn the names of the different parts of the inner mouth including the teeth.

THE TONGUE (اللسان)

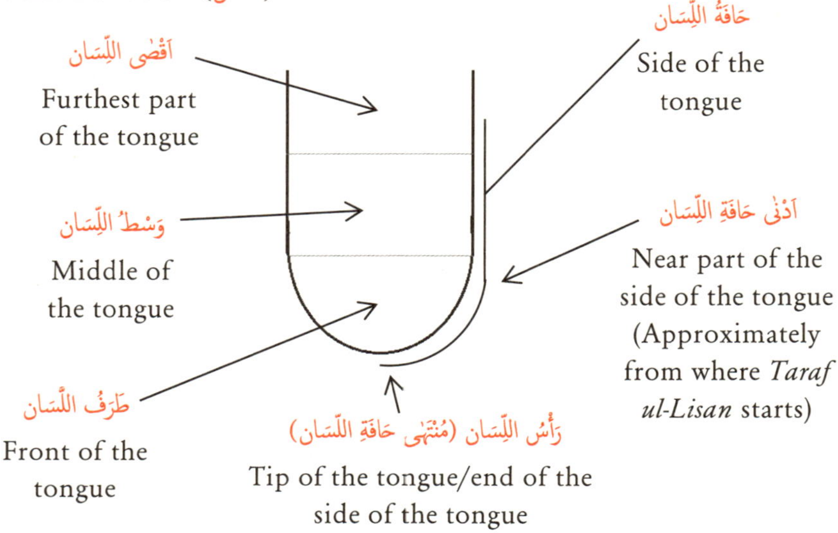

THE TEETH (الأَسْنَان)

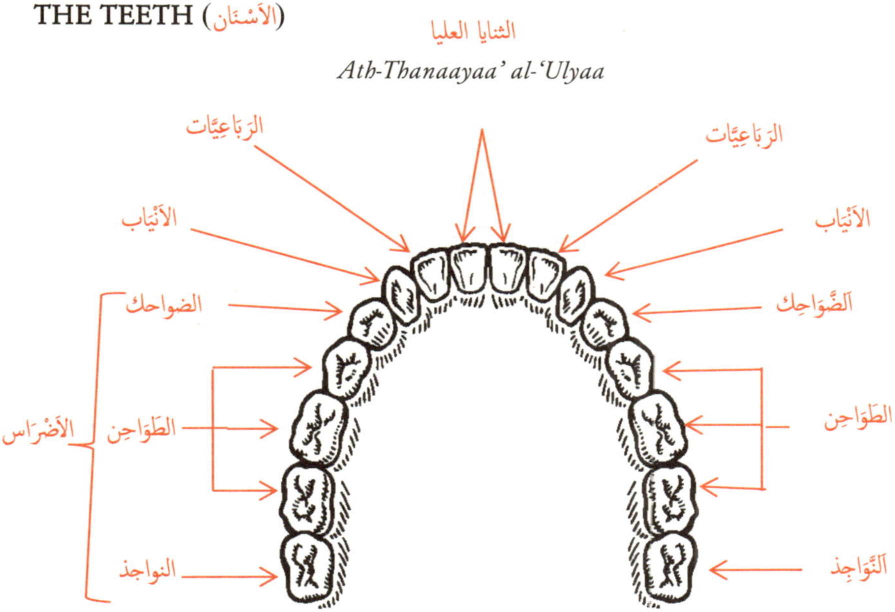

THE UPPER PALATE OF THE MOUTH اَلْحَنَكُ الأَعْلَى

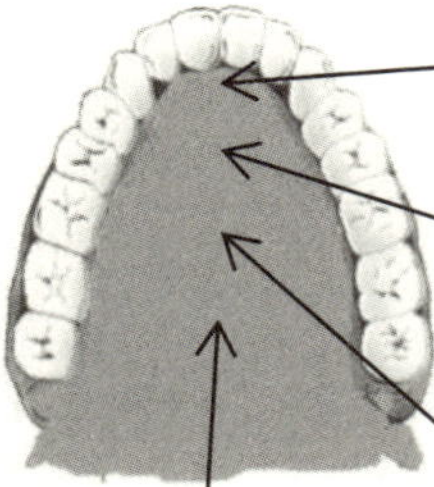

اَللِّثَةُ the Gum

مُقَدَّمُ الْحَنَك This is the front upper palate above *Taraf ul-Lisan*. Also known as: نِطَعُ الْحَنَك

اَلْحَنَكُ الْعَظْمِيُّ This is the bony upper palate, which is above *Wast ul-Lisan*. Also referred to as: الحَنَكُ الصُّلْبُ

اَلْحَنَكُ اللَّحْمِيُّ This is the soft upper palate, which is directly above *Aqsa al-Lisan*. Also known as: الحَنَكُ الرِّخْوَةُ

Fifth *Makhraj* – *Aqsal Lisan* and *Al-Hanak ul-Lahmi*

This is the *Makhraj* for the letter *Qaf* (ق), which is pronounced by raising *Aqsal Lisan* to *Al-Hanak ul-Lahmi* (The upper soft palate).

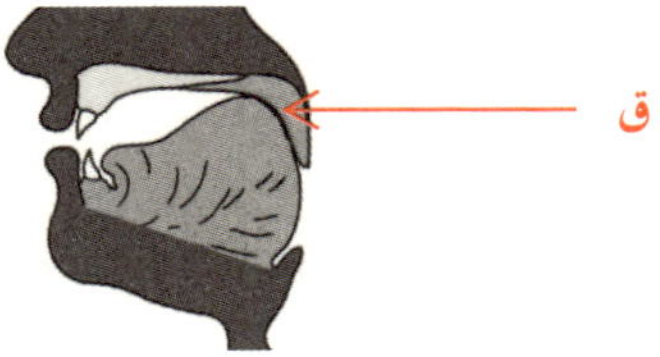

Sixth *Makhraj* – *Aqsal Lisaan* and *Al-Hanak ul-Lahmi,* but just in front of the *Makhraj* of the *Qaf* towards *Al-Hanak ul-'Azmi.*

This is the *Makhraj* for the letter *Kaf* (ك), which is pronounced by raising *Aqsal Lisan* to *Al-Hanak ul-Lahmi* (the upper soft palate), but more towards the front, near to *Al-Hanak ul-'Azmi* (the upper hard palate).

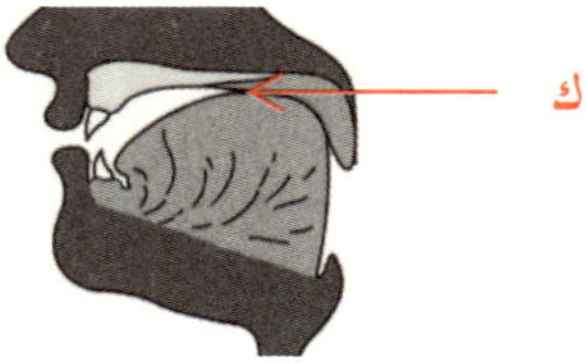

In line 12 and 13 *Ibn al-Jazari* (رضي الله عنه) mentions the *Makharij* of *Qaf* and *Kaf*:

[12] ..... وَ [مَخْرَجُ] الْقَاف ... أَقْصَى اللِّسَانِ [وَمَا] فَوْق [ذلك مِنَ الْحَنَكِ الْأَعْلَى] ثُمَّ الْكَافُ

..and the Qaf...

...Is from the furthest part of the tongue [raised] to the palate above, then the Kaf...

[13] أَسْفَلُ [مِنَ الْقَافِ]..................................

...Is lower [than the Qaf]..

Seventh *Makhraj* – *Wast ul-Lisan* and *Al-Hanak ul-'Azmi*

This is the *Makhraj* for the following three letters:
Jeem (ج)
Sheen (ش)
Ya (ي)
They are pronounced by raising *Wast ul-Lisan* to *Al-Hanak ul-'Azmi* (the upper hard palate of the mouth).

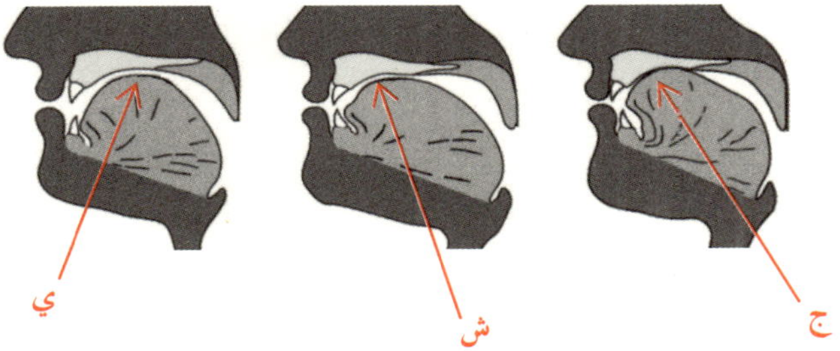

Note: When pronouncing the letter *Jeem*, the air flow stops, but with the letters *Sheen* and *Ya* some of the air flows through the middle of the tongue. Observe the following diagram for *Sheen* and *Ya*:

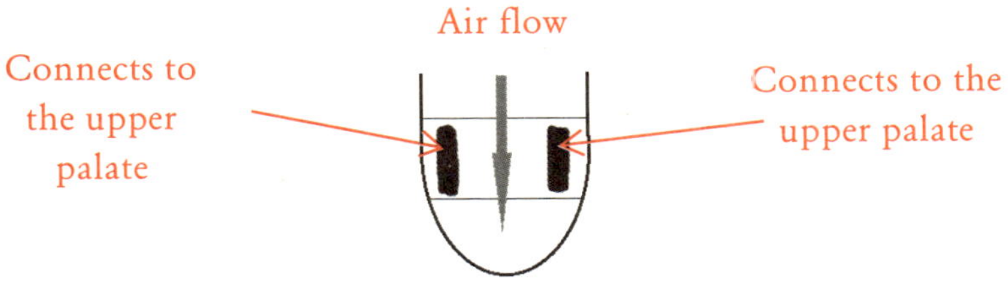

Ibn al-Jazari ﷺ mentions the *Makharij* of the three letters in line 13:

[13] ..... وَالْوَسْطُ فَجِيمُ الشِّينُ يَا ... .

(اي وَسْطُ اللِّسَانِ فَمَخْرَجُ الْجِيْمِ وَ الشِّيْنِ وَ الْيَاءِ)

... And the middle [of the tongue is the Makhraj for] Jeem, Sheen and Ya

Eighth *Makhraj* – The left or right side of *Haafat ul-Lisan* and *Al-Adhras,*

This is the *Makhraj* for the letter *Dhad* (ض), which is pronounced by raising the left or right side of *Hafat ul-Lisaan* to *Al-Adhras* (Molar teeth).

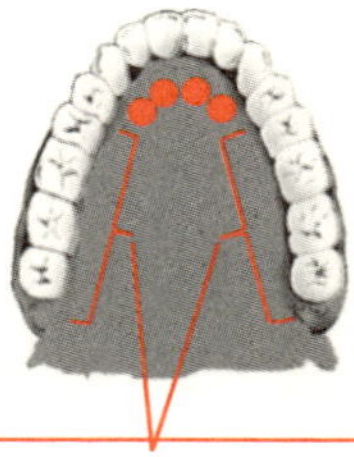

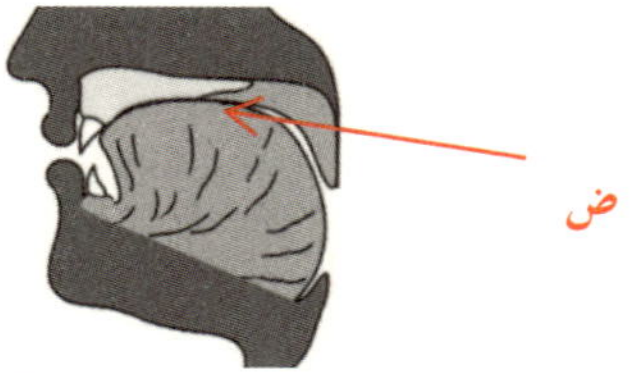

The left or right side of *Hafat ul-Lisan* will apply pressure in the inside edge of the *Al-Adhras* teeth and the front part of the tongue will also touch the dotted area without pressure.

Imam Ibn al-Jazari ﷺ says in line 13 and 14:

[13] .... وَالضَّادُ مِنْ حَافَتِهِ (اي حَافَةِ اللِّسَانِ) إِذْ وَلِيَا

And the Dhad is from its edge, when it meets…

[14] الاضْرَاسَ مِنْ أَيْسَرَ أَوْ يُمْنَاهَا ... .

With the molar teeth, from its left or right side

Ninth *Makhraj* – From the left side of *Adna Hafat il-Lisan* until the right side *Adna Hafat il-Lisan* and the gums of the upper teeth.

This is the *Makhraj* for the letter *Laam* (ل), which is pronounced by connecting the left side of *Adna Hafat il-Lisan* until the right side *Adna Hafat il-Lisan* to the gums of the upper teeth.

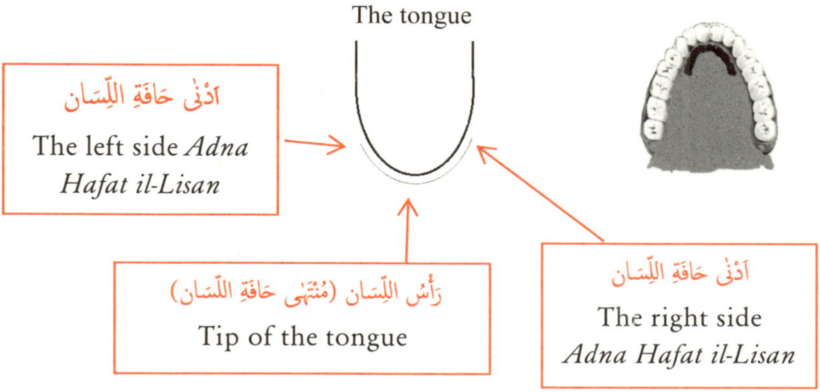

Concerning *Laam*, *Imam Ibn al-Jazari* ﵁ says in line 14:

[14] .... وَاللاَّمُ [مِنْ] أَدْنَاهَا (اي أَدْنٰى حَافَةِ اللِّسَان) لِمُنْتَهَاهَا (اي مُنْتَهَى حَافَةِ اللِّسَانِ)

And Laam is from its Adna (near edge) until its end (i.e. tip of the tongue) from both sides

Tenth *Makhraj* – *Taraf ul-Lisan* and the *Lithah* (gums) of the upper teeth.

This is the *Makhraj* for the letter *Nun* (ن), which is pronounced by connecting *Taraf ul-Lisan* to the *Lithah* of the upper *Thanaayaa'* teeth.

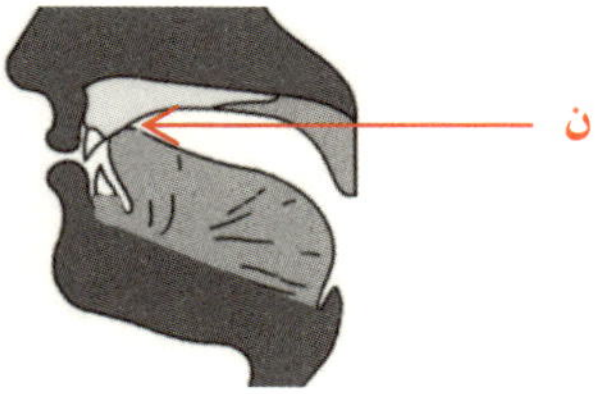

Line 15 says:

[15] وَالنُّونُ مِنْ طَرْفِهِ (اي طَرَفِ اللِّسَانِ) تَحْتُ اجْعَلُوا

(اي اِجْعَلُواهَا تَحْتَ اللَّامِ قَلِيْلًا) ......

And the Nun is from its Taraf (i.e. Taraf ul-Lisan), make it lower [than Laam]

The Difference Between the *Makhraj* of *Laam* and *Nun*

Imam Ibn al-Jazari has indicated to one of the differences between *Nun* and *Laam*, by saying 'make it lower than *Laam'*, i.e. slightly closer to the *Thanaayaa* compared to the *Laam*. The other differences between the two are:

1. *Laam* is pronounced using the *Hafat ul-Lisan*, whereas, the *Nun* is pronounced using *Taraf ul-Lisan*.
2. Air does not flow through the *Khayshum* in *Laam*, but when pronouncing the *Nun* some of the air will flow through the *Khayshum*.
3. It is also said that the amount of contact of the tongue with the *Lithah* is different in both. Observe the diagram below:

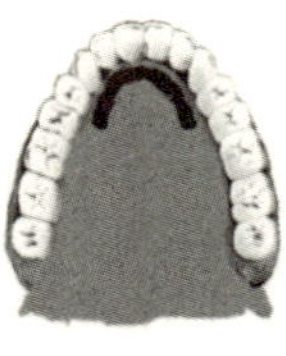

Laam: The *Hafah* is touching the *Lithah* (Gums) of the following teeth:

1. *Ath-Thanaayaa*
2. *Ar-Raba'iyaat*
3. *Al-Anyaab*
4. *Ad-Dhawahik*

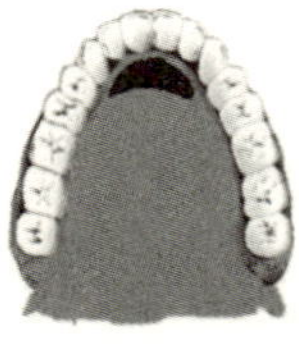

Nun: The *Taraf ul-Lisan* is touching the *Lithah* (Gums) of the following teeth:

1. *Ath-Thanaayaa*
2. *Ar-Raba'iyaat*
3. *Al-Anyaab*

Eleventh *Makhraj* – *Taraf ul-Lisan* and the *Lithah* (gums) of the upper teeth.

This is the *Makhraj* for the letter *Ra* (ر), which is pronounced by connecting *Taraf ul-Lisan* to the *Lithah* of the upper *Thanaayaa'*, but slightly further in *Zhahr ul-Lisan* compared to the *Nun*.

[15] .... وَالرَّا يُدَانِيهِ لِظَهْرٍ أَدْخَلُ (اي أَنَّهَا أَدْخَلُ في ظَهْرِ اللِّسَانِ مِنَ النُّونِ قَلِيْلًا)

And the Ra is close to it (i.e. Nun), but further in Zhahr ul-Lisan

Note: *Zhahr ul-Lisan* is the complete top surface of the tongue, which can be divided into the following sections: *Aqsa al-Lisan, Wast ul-Lisan, Taraf ul-Lisan* and *Ra's ul-Lisan*.

Although, the *Makhraj* of the *Ra* is after the *Makhraj* of the *Nun*, but the area of *Zhahr ul-Lisan* used for the letter *Ra* extends further into the mouth in comparison to the letter *Nun*. Therefore, a greater part of the *Zhahr ul-Lisan* is used for the letter *Ra* compared to the letter *Nun*.

Note: Another difference between the *Nun* and *Ra* is that the front of the tongue is closed in *Nun*, so all of the air comes out of the *Khayshum*. On the other hand, there should be a small gap for air to pass when pronouncing the letter *Ra*.

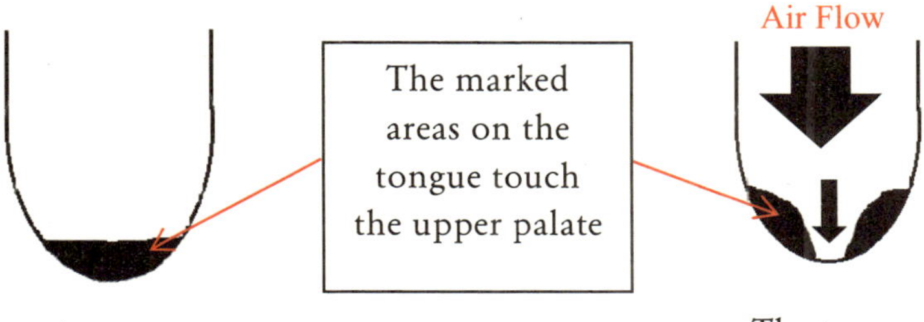

The tongue in *Nun*

The tongue in *Ra*

Twelfth *Makhraj* – *Taraf ul-Lisan* and the roots of the upper *Thanaayaa'*.

This is the *Makhraj* for three letters: *Ta* (ت), *Ta* (ط) and *Dal* (د). They are pronounced by connecting *Taraf ul-Lisan* with the roots of the upper *Thanaayaa'*, as opposed to the gums. Therefore, the tip of the tongue will touch the inside of upper *Thanaayaa'*, whereas in the previous *Makharij* that did not happen.

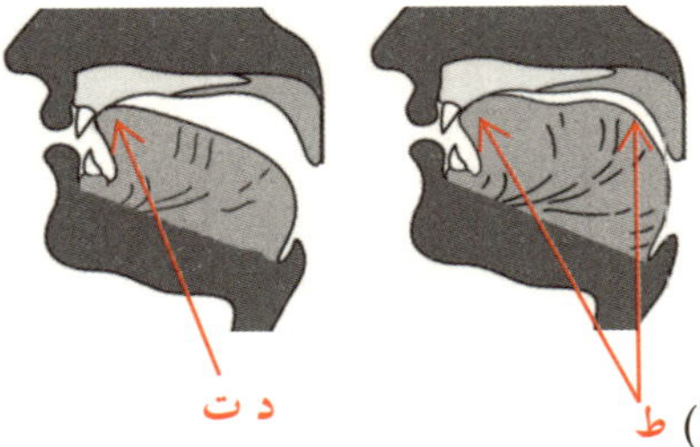

(Back of the tongue is raised)

In line 16, *Imam Ibn al-Jazari* ﷺ mentions the *Makhraj* of the three letters as follows:

[16] والطاء والدال وتا منه (اي مِنْ طَرَفِ اللِّسَانِ) وَمِنْ ... عُلْيَا الثَّنَايَا (اي الثَّنَايَا الْعُلْيَا)

And Ta, Dal and Ta are from it (i.e. Taraf ul-Lisan) and from..
...The [roots of the] upper incisor teeth, ...

Thirteenth *Makhraj* – *Ra's ul-Lisan* and the lower *Thanaayaa'*.

This is the *Makhraj* for three *Safeer* letters: *Zay* (ز), *Seen* (س) and *Saad* (ص). They are pronounced by keeping *Ra's ul-Lisaan* just above the lower *Thanaayaa'*, but not touching. This narrows the gap producing a whistle sound.

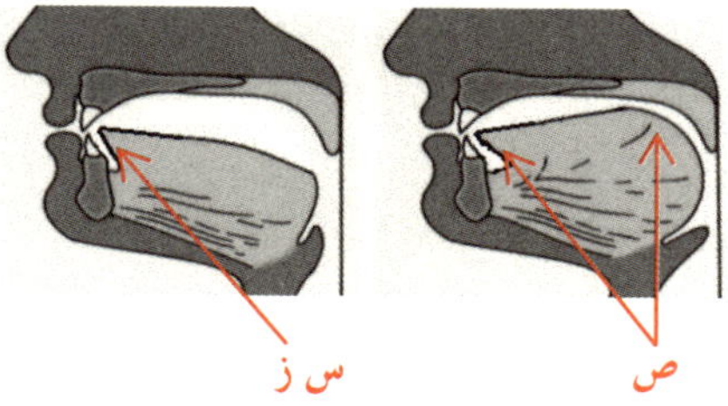

Line 16 and 17 mentions the *Makhraj* of the *Safeer* letters as follows:

[16] .... و الصفير مُسْتَكِنْ

and the Safeer letters are established...

[17] مِنْهُ وَمِنْ فَوْقِ الثَّنَايَا السُّفْلَى ... .

...From it (i.e. Ra's ul-Lisan) and from above the lower incisors

Fourteenth *Makhraj* – *Taraf ul-Lisan* and the edge of the upper *Thanaayaa'* (Incisors).

This is the *Makhraj* for the following three letters:
Zha (ظ) , *Zhal* (ذ) and *Tha* (ث)

They are pronounced by connecting the *Taraf ul-Lisan* with the edge of the upper *Thanaayaa'*, as shown in the following diagram:

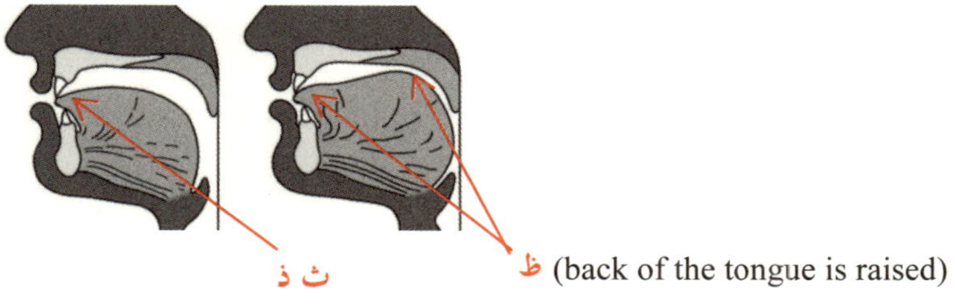

Line 17 and 18 from the poem says:

[17] .... وَالظَّاءُ وَالذَّالُ وَثَا لِلْعُلْيَا (اي مَخْرَجُ الظَّاءِ وَ الذَّالِ وَ الثَّاءِ خَاصٌ لِلثَّنَايَا الْعُلْيَا)

And Zha, Zhal, and Tha are from the upper [incisors]...

[18] مِنْ طَرَفَيْهِمَا (اي من طَرَفَيْ اللِّسَانِ وَ الثَّنَايَا)

...From both of their edges (i.e. the edge of the tongue and the teeth)

Fifteenth *Makhraj* – Inside of the lower lip connected with the edge of the upper *Thanaayaa'* (Incisors).

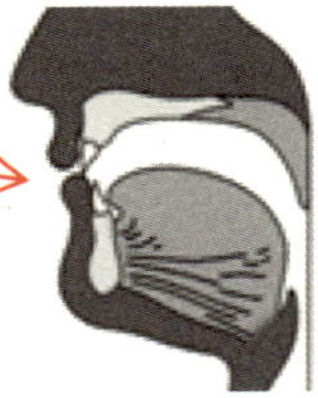

This is the *Makhraj* of the letter *Fa* (ف), which *Imam Ibn al-Jazari* describes as follows:

[18] ...... وَمِنْ بَطْنِ الشَّفَهْ ... فَالْفَا [تَخْرُجُ] مَعَ اطْرافِ الثَّنَايَا الْمُشْرِفَهْ (اي الثَّنَيَا الْعُلْيَا)

.... and from the inside of the [lower] lip...
...the Fa [is pronounced] with the edges of the noble (i.e. upper) incisors

Sixteenth *Makhraj* – Both lips

This is the *Makhraj* of *Waw* (و), *Ba* (ب), *and Mim* (م), which *Imam Ibn al-Jazari* ﷺ mentions as follows:

[19] لِلشَّفَتَيْنِ الْوَاوُ بَاءٌ مِيْمُ (اي مَخْرَجُ الْوَاوِ وَ الْبَاءِ وَ الْمِيْمِ خَاصٌ لِلشَّفَتَيْنِ)...

From both lips are Waw, Ba and Mim.

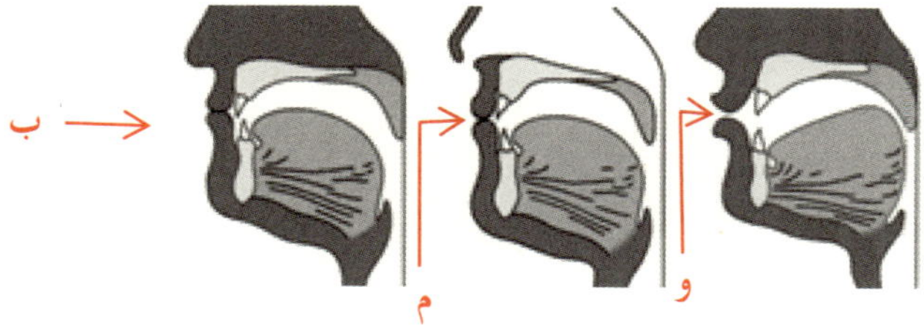

Note: *Waw* is pronounced by making the lips circular, unlike *Ba* and *Mim*.

Seventeenth *Makhraj* – *Khayshum* (Nasal Cavity)

This is the *Makhraj* of *Ghunnah*. *Imam Ibn al-Jazari* writes:

[19] .... وَغُنَّةٌ مَخْرَجُهَا الخَيْشُومُ

.... And Ghunnah, its point of articulation is the nasal cavity.

Did you know

روي أن ابا حنيفة رحمه الله تعالى ناظر معتزليا فقال له: قل با فقال با ثم قال قل خا فقال خا , فقال له بيّن مخرجهما فبينهما فقال إن كنتَ خالق فعلك فأخرج الباء من مخرج الخاء فبهت المعتزلي (المنح الفكرية شرح الجزرية لملا على القاري)

It is narrated that *Imam Abu Hanifah* once debated a *Mu'tazili*, who believed that humans create their own actions and not Allah.

Imam Abu Hanifah asked him to pronounce the letter *Ba*, which the *Mu'tazili* did. *Imam Abu Hanifah* then asked him to pronounce the letter *Kha*, which he did. *Imam Abu Hanifah* then asked him to clarify the *Makharij* of both letters. The *Mu'tazili* was able to do so.

Then *Imam Abu Hanifah* said 'if you are the creator of your own actions, then create the letter *Ba* from the *Makhraj* of *Kha*! The *Mu'tazali* was dumbfound.

(*Al-Minah al-Fikriyyah, Mulla Ali alQari*)

باب صفات الحروف

Attributes of Letters

[20] صِفَاتُهَا جَهْرٌ وَّرِخْوٌ مُّسْتَفِلْ ... مُنْفَتِحٌ مُّصْمَتَةٌ وَّالضِّدَّ قُلْ

[21] مَهْمُوسُهَا (فَحَثَّهُ شَخْصٌ سَكَتْ) ... شَدِيْدُهَا لَفْظُ (أَجِدْ قَطٍ بَكَتْ)

[22] وَبَيْنَ رِخْوٍ وَّالشَّدِيدِ (لِنْ عُمَرْ) ... وَسَبْعُ عُلْوٍ (خُصَّ ضَغْطٍ قِظْ) حَصَرْ

[23] وَصَادُ ضَادٌ طَاءُ ظَاءٌ مُّطْبَقَهْ ... وَ (فِرَّ مِنْ لُبِّ) الْحُرُوفِ الْمُذْلَقَهْ

[24] صَفِيرُهَا صَادٌ وَّ زَايٌ سِينُ ... قَلْقَلَةٌ (قُطْبُ جَدٍّ) وَّاللِّينُ

[25] وَاوٌ وَّ يَاءٌ سَكَنَا وَانْفَتَحَا ... قَبْلَهُمَا وَالْاِنْحِرَافُ صُحِّحَا

[26] فِي اللَّامِ وَالرَّا وَ بِتَكْرِيرٍ جُعِلْ ... وَلِلتَّفَشِّي الشِّيْنُ ضَادًا اسْتَطِلْ

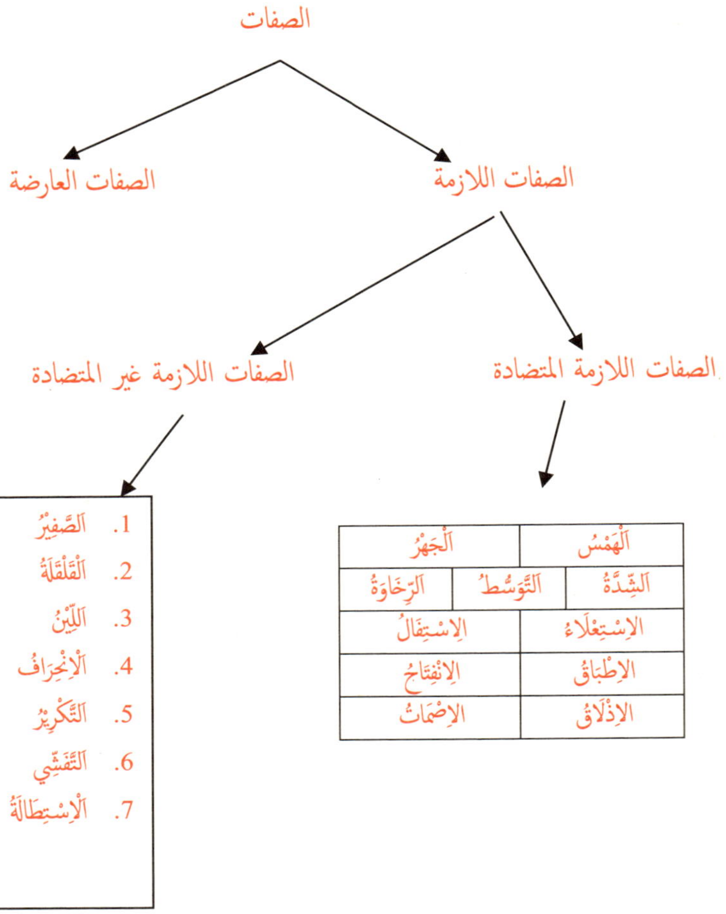
الصفات
الصفات اللازمة
الصفات العارضة
الصفات اللازمة المتضادة
الصفات اللازمة غير المتضادة
اَلْهَمْسُ
اَلْجَهْرُ
اَلشِّدَّةُ
اَلتَّوَسُّطُ
اَلرِّخَاوَةُ
اَلِاسْتِعْلَاءُ
اَلِاسْتِفَالُ
اَلِاطْبَاقُ
اَلِانْفِتَاحُ
اَلِاذْلَاقُ
اَلِاصْمَاتُ
1. اَلصَّفِيْرُ
2. اَلْقَلْقَلَةُ
3. اَللِّيْنُ
4. اَلْاِنْحِرَافُ
5. اَلتَّكْرِيْرُ
6. اَلتَّفَشِّي
7. اَلْاِسْتِطَالَةُ

THE PERMANENT ATTRIBUTES THAT HAVE OPPOSITES

There are five *Sifaat* that also have opposites to them. *Imam Ibn al-Jazari* ﷺ mentions them in line 20:

[20] صِفَاتُهَا (اي صِفَاتُ الْحُرُوفِ) جَهْرٌ وَ رِخْوٌ [وَ] مُسْتَفِلْ ...[وَ] مُنْفَتِحٌ[وَ] مُصْمَتَةٌ

Their Sifaat are Jahr, Rikhwa, Mustafil
Munfatih, Musmatah..............................

Note: In order to preserve the rhythmic pattern of the poem, at times the author uses the root word (*Masdar*), such as جَهْرٌ , and at times the adjective, such as مُسْتَفِلْ , to indicate to the *Sifaat*.

The First *Sifah*: الجهر (*Al-Jahr*)

This is the stoppage or the struggle of breath at the *Makhraj*, to the extent that the vibrations of the air struggling can be felt in the throat using the finger tips.

اِنْحِبَاسُ جَرْيَانِ النَّفَسِ عِنْدَ النُّطْقِ بِالْحَرْفِ

"The blockage in flow of breath when pronouncing the letter."

Note: it is not the case that the air flow will completely stop for each letter that has *Jahr*. In some letters, like *Jeem*, it completely stops, whilst in others the air flow struggles causing the throat to vibrate, like the letter *Waw*.

All Arabic letters have *Jahr* **except** the following:

فَحَثَّهُ شَخْصٌ سَكَتْ (ف ح ث ه ش خ ص س ك ت)

The Second *Sifah*: الرخاوة (*Ar-Rikhawah*)

This is the continuation of sound, regardless of whether or not the breath struggles.

جَرْيَانُ الصَّوْتِ عِنْدَ النُّطْقِ بِالْحَرْفِ

"The continuation of sound when pronouncing the letter."

All letters have *Rikhawah* **except** the following 13 letters:

أَجِدْ قَطٍ بَكَتْ (أ ج د ق ط ب ك ت)
لِنْ عُمَر (ل ن ع م ر)

The Third *Sifah*: الاستفال (*Al-Istifal*)

This is lowering the back of the tongue, to produce an empty sound. A letter which has *Istifal* is called *Mustafil*.

إنْخِفَاضُ اللِّسَانِ إلى قَاعِ الْفَمِ عِنْدَ النُّطْقِ بِحُرُوْفِه

"Lowering the [back of the] tongue towards the floor on the mouth, when pronouncing the letter."

Every letter has *Istifal* **except** the following 7 letters:

خُصَّ ضَغْطٍ قِظْ (خ ص ض غ ط ق ظ)

The Fourth *Sifah*: الانفتاح (*Al-Infitah*)

This is keeping the tongue away from the upper palate of the mouth (*Al-Hanak ul-A'la*), so that the air flows without being trapped between the tongue and the upper palate. A letter which has *Infitah* is called *Munfatih*.

إفْتِرَاقُ اللِّسَانِ عَنِ الْحَنَكِ الأَعْلى بِحَيْثُ يَخْرُجُ الْهَوَاءُ مِنْ بَيْنِهِمَا عِنْدَ النُّطْقِ بِحُرُوْفِه

"Separating the tongue from the upper palate in a manner that air passes from between them when pronouncing the letters."

All letters have *Infitah* **except** the following 4:

ص ض ط ظ

The Fifth *Sifah*: الاصمات (*Al-Ismaat*)

Every letter has *Ismaat* **except** for the following 6 letters:

فِرَّ مِنْ لُبِّ (ف ر م ن ل ب)

Ismaat literally means prevention and *Ibn Yalusha* describes the reason why all letters **except** the above 6 are called *Musmatah* (مُصْمَتَةٌ), 'the prevented':

وَ لُقِبَتْ بِذلك لِأَنها مُنِعَتْ مِنَ الْإِفْرَاد وحدها بِكَلِمَةٍ رُباعيةٍ فَأَكْثَرَ في كَلامِ العربِ لِثِقْلِهَا عَلى اللسان فلا تُوجَدُ كلمةٌ رُبَاعِيَّةٌ فَأَكْثَرَ في كلامهم إلا وفيها حرف مُذْلَقٌ لِلتَّعادُلِ

"These are labelled with Ismaat, because they are prevented from forming a four or more lettered word by themselves in the Arabic language, due to their heaviness and difficulty in pronunciation. So, there isn't a four or more lettered word in the Arabic language, except that it contains a letter of Izlaaq in order to balance the word."

In other words, these are letters that are not as easy to pronounce as the *Izlaaq* letters, which are mentioned later in this section. The difficulty in pronouncing them arises due to their *Makharij* being those parts of the mouth and tongue, which are not very flexible. This is why four and five lettered Arabic words are never composed exclusively of *Ismaat* letters. They will definitely have at least one *Izlaaq* letter to make their pronunciation easier. Thus, *Ismaat* is described as:

ثِقْلُ الْحَرْفِ وَ عَدَمُ سُرْعَةِ النُّطْقِ بِه

"The heaviness of a letter and the inability of it being pronounced quickly."

THE OPPOSITES

The Opposite of *Jahr:* الهمس (*Al-Hams*)

This is the continuation of breath without any struggle. Hence, vibrations cannot be felt in the throat. A letter which has *Hams* is called *Mahmusah*. The *Mahmusah* letters are ten:

فَحَثَّهُ شَخْصٌ سَكَتْ (ف ح ث ه ش خ ص س ك ت)

Imam Ibn al-Jazari ﷺ writes:

[20] .... وَالضِّدَّ قُلْ (اي أُذْكُرْ ضِدَّ هذِه الْخَمْسَةِ)

..................And Say that the opposites [of them are]...

[21] مَهْمُوسُهَا (اَي الْحُرُوفُ الْمَهْمُوسَةُ) فَحَثَّهُ شَخْصٌ سَكَتْ ... .

The Mahmusah letters, [which] are فَحَثَّهُ شَخْصٌ سَكَتْ

The Opposite of *Rikhawah:* الشدة (*Ash-Shiddah*)

This is the discontinuation of sound, regardless of the breath stopping or continuing. A letter which has *Shiddah* is called *Shadeedah*. The *Shadeedah* letters are:

أَجِدْ قَطٍ بَكَتْ (أ ج د ق ط ب ك ت)

Rikhawah and *Shiddah* are unique *Sifaat*, because they have a *Sifah* in between them, called *Tawassut*, which is not a complete stoppage of sound like *Shiddah* and nor a complete flow like *Rikhawah*. The letters that have *Tawassut* are the following five letters:

لِنْ عُمَر (ل ن ع م ر)

Imam Ibn al-Jazari ﷺ says:

[21] ... شَدِيْدُهَا لَفْظُ أَجِدْ قَطٍ بَكَتْ (اي خُذِ الْحُرُوفَ الشَّدِيْدَةَ مِنْ لَفْظِ أَجِدْ قَطٍ بَكَتْ)

The Shadeedah letters are أَجِدْ قَطٍ بَكَتْ

[22] وَبَيْنَ رِخْوٍ وَالشَّدِيدِ [خَمْسَةُ أَحرُفٍ يَجْمَعُهَا قَوْلُكَ] لِنْ عُمَرْ ... .

and between Rikhwa and Shadeed are the لِنْ عُمَرْ *[letters]*

The Opposite of *Istifal:* الاستعلاء *(Al-Isti'la)*

This is raising the back of the tongue to create a full-mouth sound. A letter which has *Isti'la* is called *Musta'liyah*. The *Musta'liyah* letters are:

خُصَّ ضَغْطٍ قِظْ (خ ص ض غ ط ق ظ)

[22] .... وَسَبْعُ عُلْوٍ خُصَّ ضَغْطٍ قِظْ حَصَرْ

(اي الحُرُوفُ الْمُسْتَعْلِيَةُ سَبْعَةٌ حَصَرَ هَا لَفْظُ خُصَّ ضَغْطٍ قِظْ)

And the seven elevated [letters] are limited to خُصَّ ضَغْطٍ قِظْ

The Opposite of *Infitah:* الاطباق *(Al-Itbaaq)*

This is trapping the sound of the letters between the tongue and the upper palate of the mouth, by raising the tongue. A letter which has *Itbaaq* is called *Mutbaqah*. The *Mutbaqah* letters are:

ص ض ط ظ

Imam Ibn al-Jazari ﷺ writes:

[23] وَصَادُ ضَادٌ طَاءُ ظَاءٌ مُطْبَقَةْ ... .

and Saad, Dhad, Ta, Zha are Mutbaqah

The Opposite of *Ismaat:* الاذلاق (*Al-Izlaaq*)

This is pronouncing the letters using *Taraf ul-Lisan* or the lips. These letters are easy to pronounce, because they are pronounced using two of the most flexible parts of the mouth. Another word for *Taraf* is *Zalaq*, which is why the letters that are pronounced using the *Taraf* are called *Muzlaqah*. The *Muzlaqah* letters are:

فِرَّ مِنْ لُبِّ (ف ر م ن ل ب)

Imam Ibn al-Jazari ؒ writes:

[23] .... وَ فِرَّ مِنْ لُبِّ الحُرُوفِ المُذْلَقَهْ

And فِرَّ مِنْ لُبِّ *letters are Al-Huruf al-Muzlaqah*

SUMMARY OF THE PERMANENT SIFAAT WITH OPPOSITES

<table>
<tr><td colspan="2">الهمس
فَحَثَّهُ شَخْصٌ سَكَتْ
(ف ح ث ه ش خ ص س ك ت)</td><td>الجهر
Remaining letters</td></tr>
<tr><td>الشدة
أَجِدْ قَطٍ بَكَتْ
(أ ج د ق ط ب ك ت)</td><td>التوسط
لِنْ عُمَر (ل ن ع م ر)</td><td>الرخاوة
Remaining letters</td></tr>
<tr><td colspan="2">الاستعلاء
خُصَّ ضَغْطٍ قِظْ
(خ ص ض غ ط ق ظ)</td><td>الاستفال
Remaining letters</td></tr>
<tr><td colspan="2">الاطباق
ص ض ط ظ</td><td>الانفتاح
Remaining letters</td></tr>
<tr><td colspan="2">الاذلاق
فِرَّ مِنْ لُبِّ
(ف ر م ن ل ب)</td><td>الاصمات
Remaining letters</td></tr>
</table>

PERMANENT ATTRIBUTES THAT DON'T HAVE OPPOSITES

The First *Sifah*: الصفير (*As-Safeer*)

This is the whistle sound that occurs when air passes between the lower and upper *Thanaayaa* and *Taraf ul-Lisan*. There are three letters that have *Safeer:*

ص ز س

Imam ibn al-Jazari ﷺ states:

[24] صَفِيرُهَا صَادٌ وَزَايٌ سِينُ ... .

Its Safeer (letters) are Saad, Zay and Seen

The Second *Sifah*: القلقلة (*Al-Qalqalah*)

This is the echo sound that occurs in five letters, when they are *Sakin*. The letters are:

قُطْبُ جَدٍّ (ق ط ب ج د)

The three levels of *Qalqalah*:

1. قلقلة صغرى (*Qalqalah Sughra*)

A small *Qalqalah* is performed when it appears in the middle of a word. For example:

وَ مَن يَّقْتُلْ

2. قلقلة كبرى (*Qalqalah Kubra*)

A big *Qalqalah* is performed, if it appears at the end of a word. For example:

لَمْ يَلِدْ

3. قلقلة اكبر (*Qalqalah Akbar*)

The Largest *Qalqalah* is performed, when one of its letters appears *Mushaddad* at the end of a word, which is then made *Sakin* due to *Waqf*. For example:

اَلْحَقّ

Imam Ibn al-Jazari ﷺ states:

[24] .... قَلْقَلَةٌ قُطْبُ جَدٍّ (اي اِخْتَصَّتْ حُرُوف "قُطْبُ جَدٍّ" بِالْقَلْقَلَةِ) ...

... *Qalqalah are* قُطْبُ جَدٍّ ......

The Third *Sifah*: اللين (*Al-Leen*)

This is pronouncing the letter with ease, in a manner that the tongue is not troubled by movement. It is found in two letters only: *Waw* and *Ya* when they are *Sakin* and preceded by a *Fathah*.

و ي

Imam Ibn al-Jazari ﷺ states:

[24] .... وَ [حُرُوفُ] اللِّين [اِثْنَانِ]

....and Leen are...

[25] وَاوٌ وَيَاءٌ سَكَنَا وَانْفَتَحَا ... قَبْلَهُمَا ....

(اي اِنْ سَكَنَ الْوَاوُ وَ الْيَاءُ وَ أَنْفَتَحَ مَا قَبْلَهُمَا يُسَمَّى لِيْنًا)

Waw and Ya, when Sakin and their preceding is Maftuh...

The Fourth *Sifah*: الانحراف (*Al-Inhiraaf*)

This is the deviation of sound due to the tongue blocking its path. It is found in two letters only: ل ر

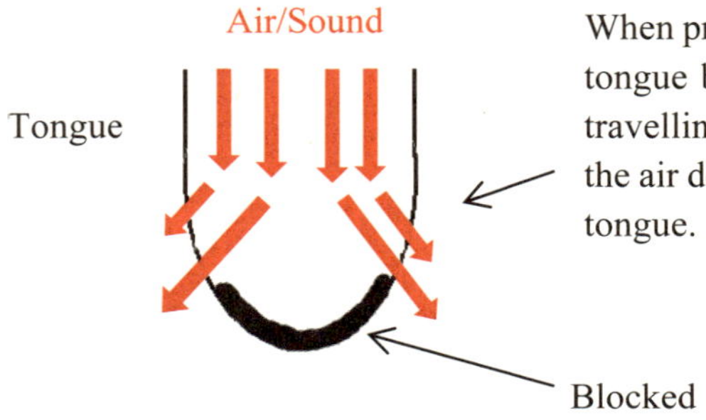

When pronouncing *Laam*, the tip of the tongue blocks the air and sound from travelling down its normal route, so, the air deviates towards the sides of the tongue.

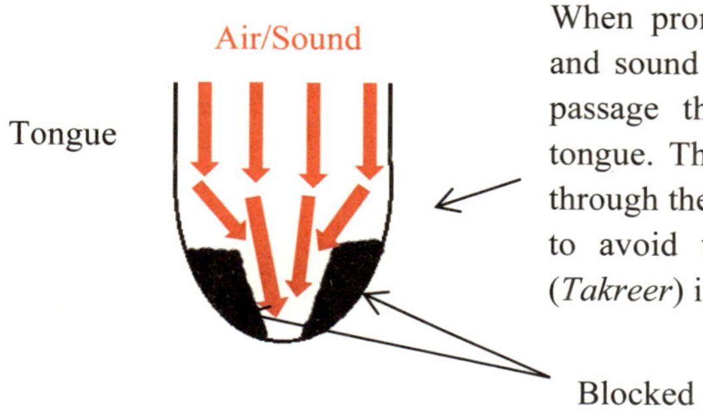

When pronouncing the letter *Ra*, air and sound is diverted down a narrow passage through the middle of the tongue. This escape of air and sound through the middle of the tongue helps to avoid the unnecessary repetition (*Takreer*) in *Ra*.

Imam Ibn al-Jazari ﷺ writes:

[25] .... وَالانْحِرَافُ صُحِّحَا

and Inhiraaf is correct...

[26] فِي اللَّامِ وَالرَّا ....

...in Laam and Ra

The Fifth *Sifah*: التكرير (*At-Takreer*)

This is the repetition of the letter *Ra*, which is also described as the rolling of the tongue. The reciter should not exaggerate it beyond what is necessary.

Imam Ibn al-Jazari ﷺ says:

[26] ..... وَ بِتَكْرِيرٍ جُعِلَ [الرَّاءُ] ... .

and with Takreer it (i.e. Ra) is made

The Sixth *Sifah*: التفشي (*At-Tafash-shi*)

This is the spreading of air in the mouth when pronouncing the letter *Sheen*. *Imam ibn al-Jazari* ﷺ says:

.... وَللتَّفَشِّي الشِّيْنُ ... .[26]

...And Tafash-shi is for Sheen....

The Seventh *Sifah*: الاستطالة (*Al-Istitalah*)

This *Sifah* has been described in different ways:

1. It is the letter *Dhad* having the longest *Makhraj*, which extends from the start of *Hafat ul-Lisan* until its end.
2. It is the lengthening of the tongue by a few millimetres in the mouth due to air pressure when pronouncing the letter *Dhad*.
3. It is the slight extension of the sound in *Dhad* due to the extension of the tongue.

Imam Ibn al-Jazari ﷺ says:

ضَادًا اسْتَطِلْ .... [26]

[and] make Dhad into Mustateel (i.e. extended)

LETTER COMPARISONS

Jeem (ج)	*Sheen* (ش)	*Ya* (ي)
Jahr	*Hams*	*Jahr*
Shiddah	*Rikhawah*	*Rikhawah*
Istifal	*Istifal*	*Istifal*
Infitah	*Infitah*	*Infitah*
Ismaat	*Ismaat*	*Ismaat*
Qalqalah	*Tafash-shi*	*Safeer*

Dhad (ض)	*Dal* (د)
Jahr	*Jahr*
Rikhawah	*Shiddah*
Isti'la	*Istifal*
Itbaq	*Infitah*
Ismaat	*Ismaat*
Istitalah	*Qalqalah*

Ta (ط)	*Ta* (ت)
Jahr	*Hams*
Shiddah	*Shiddah*
Isti'la	*Istifal*
Itbaq	*Infitah*
Ismaat	*Ismaat*
Qalqalah	

Seen (س)	*Shad* (ص)
Hams	*Hams*
Rikhawah	*Rikhawah*
Istifal	*Isti'la*
Infitah	*Infitah*
Ismaat	*Ismaat*
Safeer	*Safeer*

Ha **(ه)**	***Ha*** **(ح)**
Jahr	*Hams*
Rikhawah	*Rikhawah*
Istifal	*Istifal*
Infitah	*Infitah*
Ismaat	*Ismaat*

Jeem **(ج)**	***Dal*** **(د)**
Jahr	*Jahr*
Shiddah	*Shiddah*
Istifal	*Istifal*
Infitah	*Infitah*
Ismaat	*Ismaat*
Qalqalah	*Qalqalah*

Hamzah **(أ)**	***'Ayn*** **(ع)**
Jahr	*Jahr*
Shiddah	*Tawassut*
Istifal	*Istifal*
Infitah	*Infitah*
Ismaat	*Ismaat*

Tha **(ث)**	***Seen*** **(س)**
Hams	*Hams*
Rikhawah	*Rikhawah*
Istifal	*Istifal*
Infitah	*Infitah*
Ismaat	*Ismaat*
	Safeer

باب التجويد

Tajweed

[27] وَالْأَخْذُ بِالتَّجْوِيدِ حَتْمٌ لَّازِمُ ... مَنْ لَّمْ يُجَوِّدِ الْقُرآنَ آثِمُ

[28] لِأَنَّهُ بِهِ الْإِلٰهُ أَنْزَلاَ ... وَهَكَذَا مِنْهُ إِلَيْنَا وَصَلَا

[29] وَهُوَ أَيْضًا حِلْيَةُ التِّلاَوَة ... وَزِيْنَةُ الْأَدَاءِ وَالْقِرَاءَة

[30] وَهُوَ إِعْطَاءُ الْحُرُوفِ حَقَّهَا ... مِنْ صِفَةٍ لَهَا وَمُسْتَحَقَّهَا

[31] وَرَدُّ كُلِّ وَاحِدٍ لِّأَصْلِه ... وَاللَّفْظُ فِي نَظِيْرِه كَمِثْله

[32] مُكَمَّلًا مِنْ غَيْرِ مَا تَكَلُّف ... بِاللُّطْفِ فِي النُّطْقِ بِلاَ تَعَسُّف

[33] وَلَيْسَ بَيْنَهُ وَبَيْنَ تَرْكِه ... إِلَّارِيَاضَةُ امْرِئٍ بِفَكِّه

IMPORTANCE OF TAJWEED

Learning its rules and principles is *Fardh Kifayah*, but its application in *Qur'an* recitation is *Fardh 'Ain. Ibn al-Jazari*, stresses the importance *Ilm at-Tajweed* in the following line:

وَالأَخْذُ بِالتَّجْوِيدِ حَتْمٌ لازِمُ ... مَنْ لَمْ يُجَوِّدِ الْقُرَآنَ آثِمُ

And taking Tajweed is an absolute necessity
For the one who does not read the Quran with Tajweed is a sinner

Not reciting the *Qur'an* in accordance with the rules of *Tajweed* is a sin. However, it must be noted that, according to *Mulla 'Ali al-Qari*, there are three types of reciters:

1. Those who are able to recite the *Qur'an* correctly and do so.
2. Those who are unable to recite it properly, yet they try according to their capability to recite it correctly.
3. Those who are unable to recite properly due to lack of effort and laziness.

It is only this last category of people who are sinners, as their incorrect recitation is a result of their own deliberate negligence. Those who are capable of reciting the *Qur'an* with *Tajweed*, must do so, otherwise it is a grave sin. According *Qadhi Ayaz* in *as-Shifa*, if a person deliberately changes, increases or omits a letter in recitation, that person will no longer be a Muslim. On the other hand, if a person struggles in recitation even after exerting effort, he will receive double the reward.

It is also worth considering the types of mistakes a reciter can make, and the effects it has on the meaning of the *Qur'an*.

Major mistakes are called *al-Lahn ul-Jaliyy*, for example:

1. **Changing a letter**: For example, reading كُلْ (Eat!) instead of قُلْ (Say!). This is an easy mistake to make, since the *Makhraj* of *Kaf* and *Qaf* and very close to each other. Likewise, avoiding the *Sifah* of *Isti'la* in *Qaf* will make it sound very similar to *Kaf*, which is also a common mistake.

2. **Omitting or adding an extra *Alif*, *Waaw* or *Yaa***: For example, reading عَلَّمَا (They both taught) instead of عَلَّمَ (He taught) or reading قَالَ (He said) instead of قَالَا (They both said). Both are very common mistakes, which occur when a reciter stretches a vowel (*Harakat*) and therefore increases a *Madd* letter, as in the first example; or ignores the stretching of a *Madd* letter, as in the second example.

3. **Changing a vowel (Arabic dialectal mark)**: For example, reading أَنْعَمْتُ (I favoured) instead of أَنْعَمْتَ (You favoured). This can occur if a person recites without due diligence and concentration.

4. **Vowelizing a *Sakin* letter**: For example, reading خَلَقَنَا (He created us) instead of خَلَقْنَا (We created). Such mistakes are also common among those who tend to recite the *Qur'an* fast without being careful.

Minor mistakes are called *al-Lahn ul-Khafiyy*. These are mistakes in the temporary *Sifaat* of a letter, like not reciting the letter *Raa* with a full mouth, when it has a *Fathah* or a *Dhammah*. Such mistakes will not alter the meaning of the *Qur'an*, but they will reduce the beauty from the pronunciation.

In the next two lines *Imam Ibn al-Jazari* ﷺ highlights the reason as to why being meticulous in recitation is important.

[28] لأَنَّهُ بِهِ الإِلَهُ أَنْزَلاَ ... وَهَكَذَا مِنْهُ إِلَيْنَا وَصَلاَ

As God revealed it with it (i.e. Tajweed)
And that's how it reached us from him

[29] وَهُوَ أَيْضًا حِلْيَةُ التِّلاَوَةِ ... وَزِينَةُ الأَدَاءِ وَالْقِرَاءَةِ

And it is also the beauty of recitation
The adornment of pronunciation and reading

There is no doubt that the most preserved book is the glorious *Qur'an*. Allah ﷻ states:

إِنَّا نَحْنُ نَزَّلْنَا الذِّكْرَ وَ إِنَّا لَهُ لَحٰفِظُوْنَ

"Indeed, we revealed the Zikr (Qur'an) and we are its preservers."

Not only are the words and meanings of the *Qur'an* preserved, but also the method of its recitation, to the extent that even though there is a gap of over 1400 years between the period of the beloved Prophet ﷺ and today, yet we know precisely how each letter of the *Qur'an* was pronounced along with the attributes of those letters. Therefore, it is a mark of honour for the Muslims who can boast having the same accent as the Prophet ﷺ in Arabic. It is this very point that *Imam Ibn al-Jazari* ﷺ is referring to in lines 28 and 29 of his poem.

Imam Ibn al-Jazari ﷺ then provides a definition of *Tajweed*, which can be summarised as 'pronouncing the letters from their correct *Makhraj* with their correct permanent and temporary *Sifaat*'.

He writes:

[30] وَهُوَ إِعْطَاءُ الْحُرُوفِ حَقَّهَا ... مِنْ صِفَةٍ [لَازِمَةٍ] لَهَا وَمُستَحَقَّهَا (اي ما يَنْشَأُ عَنْ
هذِهِ الصِّفَاتِ كَترقيقٍ و تفخيمٍ و اظهارٍ و ادغامٍ و غيرِ ذلك مِن الصِّفاتِ العَارِضَةِ)

It is giving the letters their due right [from the permanent Sifaat]
and their due requirements from their [temporary] Sifaat

[31] وَرَدُّ كُلِّ وَاحِدٍ [مِنَ الحُروفِ] لأَصْلِهِ (اي مَخْرَجِه) ... .

And returning every letter back to its origin (i.e. Makhraj)

Next, *Imam Ibn al-Jazari* ﵀ explains that there needs to be consistency in recitation. For example, after a reciter has performed a *Madd* for the duration of 4 *Harakaat*, then if a similar *Madd* appears again in the recitation, the reciter should recite it the same, i.e. the second *Madd* should also be extend to the duration of 4 *Harakaat*. Likewise, when a letter is pronounced with particular qualities, it should be recited the same throughout the recitation with those same qualities each time it is repeated.

Imam Ibn al-Jazari ﵁ says:

[31] .... وَاللَّفْظُ فِي نَظِيْرِهِ كَمِثْله

(أي إذا قرأ القارئ بحرفٍ، ثم مرَّ معه غيرُه مثله، فعليه أن يَلْفِظَ بالحرفِ الثاني كما لَفَظَ بالأوّل)

And every letter [when] among it's a like, [should be pronounced] just like
it [did the first time] ...

In line 32, he explains that a reciter should aim to read and pronounce the words of the *Qur'an* with ease and love, which is only possible after the initial phase of learning that requires hard work and effort. He describes the initial phase of learning as jaw exercising, the absence of which is the only thing stopping a person from becoming a proficient reciter.

He writes:

[32] مُكَمَّلًا مِنْ غَيْرِ مَا تَكَلُّفِ ... بِاللُّطْفِ فِي النُّطْقِ بِلاَ تَعَسُّفِ

... complete, without any [undue] burden
With love in pronunciation without difficulty

[33] وَلَيْسَ بَيْنَهُ (اي بين التجويد) وَبَيْنَ تَرْكِهِ ... إِلَّارِيَاضَةُ امْرِئٍ بِفَكِّهِ

There is nothing between it (i.e. Tajweed) and leaving it
Except the exercise of a person's jaw

Did you know

The word *Tajweed* (تَجْوِيْد) is a root word (مَصْدَر) in Arabic and it means 'to beautify'. This science is called *Tajweed*, because by applying its rules a person beautifies his pronunciation of the *Qur'an*. Hence, recitation with *Tajweed* is called *Al-Qira'at al-Mujawwadah* (القِرَاءَةُ المُجَوَّدَةُ) 'the beautified recitation'.

The aim of *Tajweed* is to recite the *Qur'an* in the most beautiful manner, which is how the Messenger of Allah ﷺ and his companions, may Allah be pleased with them all, recited.

باب التفخيم و الترقيق
و بعض التنبيحات

Tafkhim, *Tarqiq* and Some Important Points

[34] فَرَقِّقَنْ مُسْتَفِلًا مِنْ أَحْرُفِ ... وَحَاذِرَنْ تَفْخِيمَ لَفْظِ الْأَلِفِ

[35] وَهَمْزِ أَلْحَمْدُ أَعُوذُ إِهْدِنَا ... اَللهِ ثُمَّ لَامِ لِلهِ لَنَا

[36] وَلْيَتَلَطَّفْ وَعَلَى اللهِ وَلَا الضْ ... وَالْمِيمِ مِنْ مَخْمَصَةٍ وَمِنْ مَرَضْ

[37] وَبَاءِ بَرْقٍ بَاطِلٍ بِهِمْ بِذِي ... فَاحْرِصْ عَلَى الشِّدَّةِ وَالْجَهْرِ الَّذِي

[38] فِيهَا وَفِي الْجِيمِ كَحُبِّ الصَّبْرِ ... رَبْوَةٍ اجْتُثَّتْ وَحَجِّ الْفَجْرِ

[39] وَبَيِّنَنْ مُقَلْقَلًا إِنْ سَكَنَا ... وَإِنْ يَكُنْ فِي الْوَقْفِ كَانَ أَبْيَنَا

[40] وَحَاءَ حَصْحَصَ أَحَطْتُ الْحَقُّ ... وَسِينِ مُسْتَقِيمِ يَسْطُوا يَسْقُوا

This section covers some important points concerning *Tarqiq*, *Tafkhim*, *Shiddah*, *Jahr*, *Qalqalah*, pronouncing the letter *Haa* with clarity and *Tarqiq*, and pronouncing the letter *Seen* with clarity and *Infitah*. The purpose of this section is to help the reader avoid the common mistakes that people make in these scenarios.

TARQIQ & TAFKHIM

A letter, which has the *Sifah* of *Isti'la*, is pronounced with a full mouth sound and this is called *Tafkhim*. On the contrary, pronouncing it with an empty mouth, due to the *Sifah* of *Istifal*, is called *Tarqiq*. The author, *Ibn al-Jazari*, ﷺ says:

[34] فَرَقِّقَنْ مُسْتَفِلًا مِنْ أَحْرُفِ ... .

Definitely make the Mustafil letters thin (i.e. empty mouth)

In other words, the letters that have the quality of *Istifal*, must always be recited with an empty mouth. However, there are three letters that are an exception to this rule, and they are the letter *Ra* (ر), *Laam* of Allah (الله) and the *Alif* (ا). These three letters oscillate between being full mouth and empty mouth. Their explanation will follow soon.

Next the Author wants the reader to be cautions with 5 letters that have *Istifal*, because they are often pronounced incorrectly.

THE ALIF

.... وَحَاذِرَنْ تَفْخِيمَ لَفْظِ الْأَلِفِ

And certainly, be cautious when making the letter Alif thick (i.e. full mouth)

The *Alif* depends upon the letter before it. So, if the letter before the *Alif* is full mouth, the *Alif* will also be recited with a full mouth. For example:

فِصَالًا

If the letter preceding it is an empty mouth letter, then the *Alif* is also recited with an empty mouth, for example:

وَحَالَ

For this reason, the author mentions in his other work called *Al-Nashr fi al-Qira'at al-'Ashr*:

واما الالف فالصحيح انها لاتوصَف بترقيق و لا تفخيم بل بحسب ما يتقدَّمها فانها تتَّبِعه ترقيقًا و تفخيما

"*The sound opinion is that the Alif cannot be labelled with Tarqiq and Tafkhim, rather it will be according to its preceding letter. It follows it in Tarqiq and Tafkhim.*"

THE HAMZAH

[35] وَ [حَاذِرَنَّ تَفْخِيْمَ] هَمْزِ أَلْحَمْدُ أَعُوذُ إِهْدِنَا ... اللهِ ....

And [be cautious of making] the Hamzah of أَلْحَمْدُ *,* أَعُوذُ *,* إِهْدِنَا *[and]* ... اللهِ *[full mouth]*

The *Hamzah* should always be recited with *Tarqiq*, i.e. empty mouth, irrespective of the neighbouring letters. Therefore, it is unlike the *Alif*, which changes according to the preceding.

The author has mentioned the following examples, which are places where many reciters, mistakenly, make the *Hamzah* full mouth:

The letter following the *Hamzah* has *Tarqiq*,	أَلْحَمْدُ	أَعُوذُ	إِهْدِنَا
The letter following the *Hamzah* has *Tafkhim*	أَللهُ	-	-

THE LAAM

The letter *Laam* must also be pronounced with *Tarqiq*, unless it is in the name Allah (الله). However, since it is mistakenly pronounced with a *Tafkhim*, especially when it is followed by a full mouth letter, the author warns the reader of this error:

[35] ....ثُمَّ [حَاذِرَنَّ تَفْخِيمَ] لَامِ لِلّٰهِ لَنَا

Then [be cautious of making] the [first] Laam of لِلّٰهِ *(and the Laam of)* لَنَا

[36] وَلْيَتَلَطَّفْ وَ عَلَى اللهِ وَلاَ الضْ ... .

And [the Laams of] وَلْيَتَلَطَّفْ , وَ عَلَى اللهِ *, and* وَ لَا الضْ *[full mouth]*

Irrespective of there being a full mouth or an empty mouth letter after the *Laam*, the *Laam* is always pronounced with an empty mouth.

وَلَا الضَّالِّيْنَ	عَلَى اللهِ	وَلْيَتَلَطَّفْ	لَنَا	لِلّٰهِ
In these three examples the *Laam* is followed by a full mouth letter.			In these two examples the *Laam* is followed by an empty mouth letter.	

THE MIM & BA

Although, both *Mim* and *Ba* are always empty mouth letters, many Arabs and non-Arabs make the mistake of reciting them with a full mouth, especially when they are followed by a full mouth letter. So, *Ibn al-Jazari* ﷺ warns of this mistake by saying:

[36] .... وَ[حَاذِرَنَّ تَفْخِيمَ] الْمِيمِ مِنْ مَخْمَصَةٍ وَمِنْ مَرَضْ

And [be cautious of making] the Mim of مَخْمَصَةٍ *and* مَرَضْ *[full mouth]*

[37] وَ[حَاذِرَنَّ تَفْخِيمَ] بَاءِ بَرْقٍ بَاطِلٍ بِهِمْ بِذِيْ ... .

And [be cautious of making] the Ba of بَرْقٍ , بَاطِلٍ , بِهِمْ *and* بِذِيْ *[full mouth]*

THE QUALITIES OF SHIDDAH AND JAHR

The author cautions the reader from making the letter *Ba* similar to the letter *Fa* and the letter *Jeem* similar to the letter *Sheen*, by not making the qualities of *Shiddah* and *Jahr* apparent.

He says:

[37] .... فَاحْرِصْ عَلَى الشِّدَّةِ وَالْجَهْرِ الَّذِي

... And strive to apply Shiddah and Jahr which is ...

[38] فِيهَا وَفِي الْجِيمِ كَحُبِّ الصَّبْرِ ... رَبْوَةٍ اجْتُثَّتْ وَحَجِّ الْفَجْرِ

...in it (i.e. in the Baa) and in the Jeem, for example حُبّ *,* الصَّبْر *, ...*

... رَبْوَة *,* اِجْتُثَّتْ *,* حَجّ *and* الْفَجْرِ

The letter *Jeem* and *Sheen* are from the same *Makhraj*, i.e. *Wast ul-Lisaan*. Therefore, the only thing that makes them sound different is *Shiddah* and *Jahr* from the attributes that have opposites.

	Jeem	***Sheen***
1	*Jahr*	*Hams*
2	*Shiddah*	*Rikhawah*
3	*Istifal*	*Istifal*
4	*Infitah*	*Infitah*
5	*Ismaat*	*Ismaat*
6	*Qalqalah*	*Tafash-shi*

The letters *Ba* and *Fa* are both from the lips and therefore close in *Makhraj*. But they sound different, because they differ in *Sifaat*.

	Ba	***Fa***
1	*Jahr*	*Hams*
2	*Shiddah*	*Rikhawah*
3	*Istifal*	*Istifal*
4	*Infitah*	*Infitah*
5	*Izlaaq*	*Izlaaq*
6	*Qalqalah*	

THE LEVELS OF QALQALAH

1. **Clear *Qalqalah***: If a letter of *Qalqalah* (قطب جد) has a permanent original *Sukun*, then the echo sound must be made clear. This will occur in the middle of a word and is also known as the 'Small *Qalqalah*' (صغري). For example:

يَقْطَعُوْنَ

The author ﷺ says:

[39] وَبَيِّنَنْ [حَرْفًا] مُقَلْقَلاً إِنْ سَكَنَا ... .

And make the Qalqalah clear if [the Qutbujaddin letter] is Sakin [with a permanent Sukun]

2. **Clearer *Qalqalah***: However, if the *Sukun* on the *Qalqalah* letter is at the end and *Waqf* is also done, then the echo sound needs to be clearer. This also known as the 'Big *Qalqalah*' (كبرى). For example:

وَ مَا كَسَبْ – لَمْ يَلِدْ

Ibn al-Jazari ﷺ says:

[39] .... وَإِنْ يَكُنْ فِي الْوَقْفِ كَانَ أَبْيَنَا

And if it is Sakin [with a temporary Sukun] during Waqf, then it [must be] clearer

3. **Exaggerated *Qalqalah***: *Mulla 'Ali al-Qari* ﷺ writes in his commentary, *al-Minah ul-Fikriyyah*:

ثم لا شكَّ أنه إذا تكرر حرفُ القلقلةِ مدغما تكون المبالغةُ في القلقلة متعيّنًانحو الحَقُّ

"So, there is no doubt that if the Qalqalah letter is repeated in the form of Idgham, then exaggeration in Qalqalah is specified. For example, الحَقُّ*"*

This is also known as the 'Largest *Qalqalah*' (اكبر).

THE HA (ح)

It must be pronounced clearly and with *Tarqiq,* especially when it appears *Sakinah* and it precedes a letter close to it in *Makhraj.* For example:

فَاصْفَحْ عَنْهُمْ	It is a common mistake to change the *Ha* (ح) into *'Ayn* (ع) and recite it with *Idgham.*
وَ سَبِّحْهُ	Similarly, it is a common mistake to change the *Ha* (ح) into *Ha* (ه) and recite it with *Idgham.*

Another common mistake is to pronounce the *Ha* full mouth when they are followed by a full mouth letter. For example:

حَصْحَصَ – أَحَطْتُ - الْحَقُّ

The author, *Ibn al-Jazari,* ﷺ explains:

[40] وَ [بَيِّنَنْ تَرْقِيقَ] حَاءِ حَصْحَصَ أَحَطْتُ الْحَقُّ ... .

And [make] the Ha of حَصْحَصَ *,* أَحَطْتُ *and* الْحَقُّ *[clearly thin]*

THE SEEN

When the letter *Seen* precedes a full mouth letter, it is commonly recited with *Itbaaq* and *Isti'la,* making it sound more like a *Saad* (ص).

However, this is a mistake and it should be recited clearly with *Infitah* and *Istifal.* For example:

مُسْتَقِيمٍ – يَسْطُوْنَ – يَسْقُوْنَ

Ibn al-Jazari ﷺ says:

[40] .... وَ [بَيِّنَنْ اِنْفِتَاحَ] سِينِ مُسْتَقِيمٍ يَسْطُوا يَسْقُوا

And [likewise make the Infitah of] the Seen of مُسْتَقِيمٍ *,* يَسْطُوا *and* يَسْقُوا *[clear]*

Reminder

أَنَّ رَسُولَ اللَّهِ صلى الله عليه وسلم قَالَ

إِنَّمَا مَثَلُ صَاحِبِ الْقُرْآنِ كَمَثَلِ صَاحِبِ الإِبِلِ الْمُعَقَّلَةِ إِنْ عَاهَدَ عَلَيْهَا أَمْسَكَهَا وَإِنْ أَطْلَقَهَا ذَهَبَتْ

The Messenger of Allah, may Allah bless him and grant him peace, said:

"A man who knows the *Qur'an* well is like a man who has a hobbled camel (i.e. a camel whose feet a tied in a way that it restricts movement). If he takes care of it, he keeps it, and if he lets it go, it gets away."

(*Al-Mu'atta of Imam Malik*)

باب الراءات

The letter Ra

[41] وَرَقِّقِ الرَّاءَ إِذَا مَا كُسِرَتْ ... كَذَاكَ بَعْدَ الْكَسْرِ حَيْثُ سَكَنَتْ

[42] إِنْ لَّمْ تَكُنْ مِّنْ قَبْلِ حَرْفِ اسْتِعْلَا ... أَوْ كَانَتِ الْكَسْرَةُ لَيْسَتْ أَصْلَا

[43] وَالْخُلْفُ فِي فِرْقٍ لِّكَسْرٍ يُوجَدُ ... وَأَخْفِ تَكْرِيْرًا إِذَا تُشَدَّدُ

Ibn Yalusha ﷺ in his commentary on this poem, called '*Al-Fawaid al-Mufhimah fi sharh al-Jazariyyah al-Muqaddimah*', writes:

و الاصل في الراء التفخيم و لاتُرَقَّقُ الا لموجِب

"*The original [sound] in Ra has Tafkhim (full mouth), and it is not made empty mouth except due to a cause.*"

Ibn al-Jazari ﷺ mentions two causes in this section.

Frist: When it has a *Kasrah* e.g. رِجَالٌ

He writes:

[41] وَرَقِّقِ الرَّاءَ إِذَا مَا كُسِرَتْ ... .

And make the Ra empty mouth, when it has a Kasrah

Second: When it is *Sakinah* and after a *Kasrah* e.g. فِرْعَوْنَ

He writes:

[41] .... كَذَاكَ بَعْدَ الْكَسْرِ حَيْثُ سَكَنَتْ

And likewise, after a Kasrah when it is Sakinah

There are two conditions for this cause:

a. There shouldn't be a full mouth letter after the *Ra*, otherwise the *Ra* will revert back to its original form and become full mouth e.g. أَنْذِرْ قَوْمَكَ

b. The *Kasrah* before it should not be temporary, otherwise the letter *Ra* will revert back to being full mouth, e.g. أَمِ ارْتَابُوا . The *Kasrah* on the *Mim* is temporary, since it has only come to avoid the gathering of two *Sakin* letters.

The author ﷺ mentions the two conditions as follows:

[42] إِنْ لَمْ تَكُنْ مِنْ قَبْلِ حَرْفِ اسْتِعْلَا ... أَوْ كَانَتِ الْكَسْرَةُ لَيْسَتْ أَصْلَا

So long as it does not appear before a full mouth letter
And [not is it the case] that the Kasrah is not original
(i.e. nor is it the case that the Kasrah is temporary)

THE DISPUTE IN فِرْقٍ

Finally, the author talks about the difference of opinion between scholars on the *Tarqiq* and *Tafkhim* of the letter *Ra* in the word فِرْقٍ.

Some have argued that it should be recited full mouth, because it is followed by a full mouth letter, just like أَنْذِرْ قَوْمَكَ . Others have argued that the *Kasrah* on the *Qaf* in the word فِرْقٍ has weakened its sound, and it is no longer pronounced with a complete full mouth, making it is similar to an empty mouth letter.

The author, *Ibn al-Jazari,* ﷺ writes:

[43] وَالْخُلْفُ فِي فِرْقٍ لِكَسْرٍ يُوجَدُ ... .

And the difference [of opinion] in فِرْقٍ *is due to the Kasrah that is found [on the Qaf]*

TAKRIR OF RA

It is necessary to only do *Takreer* to extent that is unavoidable, otherwise the ruling is to conceal the repetition, especially when it is *Mushaddadah*. For this reason, scholars, such as *Mulla Ali al-Qari*, have said it is *Wajib* to hide the *Takreer* in *Ra*.

[43] .... وَأَخْفِ تَكْرِيرًا إِذَا تُشَدَّدُ

And hide the Takreer, when it is Mushaddadah

Reminder

Allah, the almighty, states:

أَفَلَا يَتَدَبَّرُونَ الْقُرْآنَ أَمْ عَلَىٰ قُلُوبٍ أَقْفَالُهَا – سورة محمد (24)

"Then do they not reflect upon the Qur'an, or are there locks upon [their] hearts?"
(Surah Muhammad, verse 24)

When was the last time you opened the *Qur'an*, with the intention to understand it and act upon it?

باب اللامات و أحكام متفرقة

The letter Laam and Various Rules

[44] وَفَخِّمِ اللَّامَ مِنِ اسْمِ اللهِ ... عَنْ فَتْحٍ اَوْ ضَمٍّ كَعَبْدُ اللهِ

[45] وَحَرْفَ الْاِسْتِعْلاَءِ فَخِّمْ وَ اخْصُصَا ... اَلاِطْبَاقَ أَقْوَى نَحْوُ قَالَ وَ الْعَصَا

[46] وَبَيِّنِ الْإِطْبَاقَ مِنْ أَحَطتُ مَعْ ... بَسَطتَ وَالْخُلْفُ بِنَخْلُقكُّمْ وَقَعْ

[47] وَاحْرِصْ عَلَى السُّكُونِ فِي جَعَلْنَا ... أَنْعَمْتَ وَ الْمَغْضُوبِ مَعْ ضَلَلْنَا

[48] وَخَلِّصِ انْفِتَاحَ مَحْذُورًا عَسٰى ... خَوْفَ اشْتِبَاهِهِ بِمَحْظُورًا عَصٰى

[49] وَرَاعِ شِدَّةً بِكَافٍ وَّ بِتَا ... كَشِرْكِكُمْ وَ تَتَوَفّٰى فِتْنَتَا

THE LAAM OF ALLAH

Mulla Ali al-Qari ﷺ writes in his commentary:

ثم اللامُ أصلُها الترقيقُ عَكْسَ الراءِ عند أهلِ التحقيق فلا تفخيمَ إلا لموجِبٍ

"Then the Laam in its original form is empty mouth, contrary to the letter Ra according to the scholars of critical inquiry. So, it is not made full mouth unless due to a cause."

The *Laam* of Allah is made full mouth only if it is preceded by a *Fathah* or a *Kasrah*, otherwise it remains empty mouth:

Preceded by a *Dhammah*	عَبْدُ اللهِ	تفخيم – full mouth
Preceded by a *Fathah*	عَبْدَ اللهِ	تفخيم – full mouth
Preceded by a *Kasrah*	عَبْدِ اللهِ	ترقيق – empty mouth

The author, *Ibn al-Jazari,* ﷺ says:

[44] وَفَخِّمِ اللَّامَ مِنِ اسْمِ اللهِ ... عَنْ فَتْحٍ اَوْ ضَمٍّ كَعَبْدُ اللهِ

And make the Laam in the name of Allah full mouth…
… [after] a Fathah or a Dhammah like عَبْدُ اللهِ

LEVELS OF ISTI'LA

All of the letters of *Isti'la* are full mouth, however those that also have the quality of *Itbaaq* are clearer and stronger compared to the other *Isti'la* letters.

ص ض ط ظ	*Isti'la* is stronger than the 3 letters in the row below, because these also have the quality of *Itbaaq*.
خ غ ق	*Isti'la* is not as strong as the 4 letters in above row.

The author, *Ibn al-Jazari,* ﷺ says:

وَحَرْفَ الاِسْتِعْلاَءِ فَخِّمْ وَ اخْصُصَا ... الاِطْبَاقَ أَقْوَى نَحْوُ قَالَ وَ الْعَصَا

And make the Isti'la letters full mouth, and specify...
The Itbaaq [letters] with greater [Tafkhim], for example قَالَ *and* الْعَصَا

The level of *Isti'la* also varies inside each letter depending on how it's placed in a word. Observe the table below, they have been arranged from the strongest to the weakest:

Strongest	If the *Isti'la* letter has a *Fathah* and an *Alif* follows it	قَالَ
↓	If it has a *Fathah* and an *Alif* does not follows it	قَوْلٌ
	If it has a *Dhammah*	قُتِلَ
	If it has a *Sukun*	يَقْتُلُ
Weakest	If it has a *Kasrah*	الْمُسْتَقِيْمَ

TYPES OF IDGHAM

There are two types of *Idgham*:

ادغام تام	هُوَ إِدْرَاجُ الاولِ في الثاني ذاتًا و صفةً It is inserting the first letter, itself and its attributes, inside the second. In a manner that nothing remains of the first letter in pronunciation, neither the letter not its attributes. Therefore, it is a complete *Idgham*. For example: قَالَتْ طَّائِفَةٌ – مِن رَّبِّهِمْ In its written form the second letter is given a *Shaddah*.
ادغام ناقص	هُوَ إِدْرَاجُ الاولِ في الثاني ذاتًا لا صفةً It is merging the first letter into the second but not merging the attributes. In other words, the attributes of the first letter are still pronounced. So, it's not a complete *Idgham*. For example: مَن يَعْمَل – أَحَطتُ – بَسَطتَ In the *Qur'an* this type of *Idgham* is written differently to the complete *Idgham*. The first letter is kept empty from vowels and *Sukun*, and the second letter is not given a *Shaddah*. Note the *Ghunnah* is still present from the *Sifaat* of the *Nun* even after it has been merged into the letter *Ya* in مَن يَعْمَل.

Since in *Idgham Naqis* the attributes of the first letter are not merged into the second letter, the *Itbaaq* inside the letter *Ta* (ط) should be observed, as missing it out will cause it to sound like a *Ta* (ت) in words like أَحَطتُ and بَسَطتَ.

However, in the word نَخْلُقكُّم, there is a difference of opinion between scholars as to which type of *Idgham* it is. Thus, there is a difference of opinion over whether or not to pronounce the attribute of *Isti'la* that was inside *Qaf*.

Hence, the author says:

[46] وَبَيِّنِ الإِطْبَاقَ مِنْ أَحَطتُ مَعْ ... بَسَطتَ وَالخُلْفُ بِنَخْلُقكُّمْ وَقَعْ

And make the Itbaaq clear in أَحَطتُ *along with...*

... بَسَطتَ *and there is a difference [of opinion] in* نَخْلُقكُّمْ

COMMON MISTAKES

First, the author highlights some places where people commonly make the mistake of vowelizing a *Sakin* letter:

1. The *Sukun* of the *Laam* when it precedes a *Nun*, for example: جَعَلْنَا
2. The *Sukun* of *Nun* in the word أَنْعَمْتَ
3. The *Sukun* of the *Ghayn* in المَغْضُوبِ
4. The *Sukun* on the second *Laam* in ضَلَلْنَا

The author says:

[47] وَاحْرِصْ عَلَى [تَبْيِيْنِ] السُّكُونِ فِي جَعَلْنَا ... أَنْعَمْتَ وَ المَغْضُوبِ مَعْ ضَلَلْنَا

And be eager on [making] the Sukun [clear] in جَعَلْنَا *...*

[And in] أَنْعَمْتَ*,* المَغْضُوبِ *along with* ضَلَلْنَا

Second, he highlights the places where people neglect the attribute of *Infitah* in the letters *Zal* (ذ) and *Seen* (س), making them sound like *Zha* (ظ) and *Saad* (ص).

He says:

[48] وَخَلِّصِ انْفِتَاحَ مَحْذُورًا عَسَى ... خَوْفَ اشْتِبَاهِهِ بِمَحْظُورًا عَصَى

And clarify the Infitah [in the Zal of] مَحْذُورًا *[and seen of]* عَسَى

...[because] of the fear of making it resemble مَحْظُورًا *and* عَصَى

Third, he stresses that the attribute of *Shiddah* must be pronounced in the letters *Kaf* (ك) and *Ta* (ت), which is commonly missed out by non-native speakers.

Ibn al-Jazari ﷺ says:

[49] وَرَاعِ شِدَّةً بِكَافٍ وَ بِتَا ... كَشِرْكِكُمْ وَ تَتَوَفَّى فِتْنَتَا

And take Shiddah into consideration for Kaf and Ta
Like شِرْكِكُمْ *,* تَتَوَفَّى *and* فِتْنَةٌ

فصل في ادغام المتماثلين و المتجانسين

Idgham of Mutamaathilayn and Mutajaanisayn

[50] وَأَوَّلَىْ مِثْلٍ وَّجِنْسٍ إِنْ سَكَنْ ... أَدْغِمْ كَقُلْ رَّبِّ وَ بَلْ لَّا وَأَبِنْ

[51] فِي يَوْمِ مَعْ قَالُوا وَهُمْ وَ قُلْ نَعَمْ ... سَبِّحْهُ لَا تُزِغْ قُلُوبَ فَالْتَقَمْ

When two neighbouring letters are *Mutamaathilayn* or *Mutajaanisayn,* like two *Laams* or *Laam* and *Ra*, then the first is merged into the second, so long as the first letter is *Sakin* and the second vowelized.

The author, *Ibn al-Jazari,* ﷺ writes:

[50] وَأَوَّلَىْ مِثْلٍ وَجِنْسٍ إنْ سَكَنْ ... أَدْغِمْ كَقُلْ رَبِّ وَ بَلْ لَّا ....

If the first of the two [letters] in Mutamaathilayn and Mutajaanisayn is Sakin,
Then do Idgham, for example قُلْ رَّبِّ *and* بَلْ لَّا*.* ....

However, the author ﷺ clarifies that if the first letter is a *Madd*, then *Idgham* is not done:

[50] .... وَأَبِنْ

And don't do Idgham...

[51] فِي يَوْمِ مَعْ قَالُوا وَهُمْ ....

... [In words like] فِي يَوْمِ *[along] with* قَالُوا وَهُمْ *...*

Furthermore, *Idgham* is not done in the places indicated in the table on the next page.

Example	Reason
قُلْ نَعَمْ	The *Laam* is not merged into the *Nun*, because of the following rule mentioned by *Mulla Ali al-Qari*: لانَّ النونَ لا يُدغَم فيها شيئٌ مِمَّا أُدْغِمَتْ هي فيه من حروفِ يرملون و مرادُهم سِوى النونِ "*Because none of the letters that the Nun merges into from* يرملون *can be merged into the Nun, except the Nun.*" **Objection**: *Laam* of *Ta'rif* (ال) is merged into the *Nun* in the following examples: النَّارُ - النَّاسِ **Answer**: The *Laam* of *Ta'rif* is an exception. Since it is used a lot, the Arabs wanted to make it lighter. So, they made it smaller and lighter by doing *Idgham*.
سَبِّحْهُ	The *Ha* (ح) is not merged into the *Ha* (ه) after it, because of the following rule: الحلقيُّ لا يُدغَم في أَدْخَلَ منه و الهاءُ اَدْخَلُ من الحاءِ The throat letters cannot be merged into letters that are further in the throat compared to them. And the *Ha* (ه) is further back compared to the *Ha* (ح).
لاَ تُزِغْ قُلُوبَنَا	The *Ghayn* (غ) is not merged into the *Qaf* (ق) after it, because they are different to each other; the *Ghayn* is from the throat and the *Qaf* if from the tongue and merging the two is difficult.
فَالْتَقَمَهُ	The *Laam* is not merged into the *Ta*, because they are different in *Makharij* and *Sifaat*. They are only the same in two attributes: *Istifal* and *Infitah*, but different in every other way. So, *Idgham* is not permitted. The exception to this rule is the *Laam* of *Ta'rif*, because it is used a lot.

The author says:

[51] .... وَ [أَيِنْ] قُلْ نَعَمْ ...[وَ] سَبِّحْهُ[وَ] لَا تُزِغْ قُلُوبَ[وَ] فَالْتَقَمْ

And don't do Idgham in سَبِّحْهُ , لاَ تُزِغْ قُلُوبَنَا *and* فَالْتَقَمَهُ

Did you know

Abu Bakr Ahmad bin Muhammad bin Muhammad al-Jazari was the son of *Imam ibn al-Jazari*, who wrote a commentary on his father poem and called it:

الحواشي المفهمة في شرح المقدمة

Abu Bakr Ahmad al-Jazari passed away in the year 835 *Hijri.*

May Allah grant them both a place in the highest levels of Paradise. Amin

باب الضاد و الظاء

The letter Dhad and Zha

[52] وَالضَّادَ بِاسْتِطَالَةٍ وَّمَخْرَج ... مَيِّزْ مِنَ الظَّاءِ وَكُلُّهَا تَجِيْ

[53] فِي الظَّعْنِ ظِلِّ الظُّهْرِ عُظْمِ الْحِفْظ ... أَيْقِظْ وَأَنْظُرْ عَظْمِ ظَهْرِ اللَّفْظ

[54] ظَاهِرْ لَظَى شُوَاظُ كَظْمٍ ظَلَمَا ... أُغْلُظْ ظَلَامَ ظُفُرٍ انْتَظِرْ ظَمَا

[55] أَظْفَرَ ظَنًّا كَيْفَ جَا وَعْظٍ سِوَى ... عِضِينَ ظَلَّ النَّحْلِ زُخْرُفٍ سَوَا

[56] وَ ظَلْتَ ظَلْتُمْ وَبِرُومٍ ظَلُّوا ... كَالْحِجْرِ ظَلَّتْ شُعَرَا نَظَلَّ

[57] يَظْلَلْنَ مَحْظُورًا مَعَ الْمُحْتَظِر ... وَكُنْتَ فَظًّا وَّجَمِيْعِ النَّظَر

[58] إِلَّا بِوَيْلٍ هَلْ وَأُوْلَى نَاضِرَهْ ... وَ الْغَيْظِ لَا الرَّعْدِ وَهُوْدٍ قَاصِرَهْ

[59] وَ الْحَظِّ لَا الْحَضِّ عَلَى الطَّعَام ... وَفِي ضَنِيْنٍ الْخِلَافُ سَامِيْ

DHAD (ض) AND ZHA (ظ)

Many reciters of the *Qur'an*, especially non-native speakers of Arabic, often make the mistake of reciting the *Dhad* as a *Zha*. So, it is important to recognise the difference between the two.

THE DIFFERENCE IN SIFAAT

The mistake of mixing the two is due to them being very close in *Sifaat* and the only difference being the *Sifah* of *Istitalah* in *Dhad*:

	Dhad	***Zha***
1	*Jahr*	*Jahr*
2	*Rikhawah*	*Rikhawah*
3	*Isti'la*	*Isti'la*
4	*Itbaq*	*Itbaq*
5	*Ismaat*	*Ismaat*
6	*Istitalah*	

Since this is a very common mistake, even amongst Arabs, the scholars have given it a lot of consideration in their books. The author has compiled seven couplets in this poem, which contain all of the words in the *Qur'an* that contain the letter *Zha*. This is in order to help the reciter differentiate it from the letter *Dhad*.

THE DIFFERENCE IN MAKHRAJ

Dhad	***Zha***
This is pronounced by using the *Hafat ul-Lisan* and the Molar teeth.	This is pronounced by using *Taraf ul-Lisan* and the edge of the upper *Thanaayaa* teeth.

The author, *Ibn al-Jazari*, ﷺ says:

[52] وَالضَّادَ بِاسْتِطَالَةٍ وَمَخْرَجِ ... مَيِّزْ مِنَ الظَّاءِ .....

As for the Dhad, using Istitalah and [its] Makhraj...
... differentiate [it] from Zha.

THE DIFFERENCE IN WRITING

The only difference between the two is that the *Zha* has an *Alif* on it which the *Dhad* does not have. This similarity also explains why many people often muddle the two letters. Observe the difference between them in the following diagram:

Hence, the letter *Zha* is called *al-Zha al-Mushalah* (الظاء المشالة), 'the carried *Zha*', because it is carried by an *Alif*. Whilst the letter *Dhad* is called *al-Dhad al-Saaqitah* (الضاد الساقطة), 'the dropped *Dhad*', because it has been dropped by the *Alif* and at times it is called *al-Dhad al-Qaasirah* (الضاد القاصرة) 'the short *Dhad*', because it is not tall like the *Zha*, as it does not have an *Alif*. The author indicates to this difference in line 58 of this poem.

ZHA IN THE QUR'AN:

In order to help the reader in distinguishing between *Dhad* and *Zha* in the *Qur'an*, the author, *Ibn al-Jazari*, ﵀ lists all of the words in the *Qur'an* that contain the letter *Zha*. However, it must be remembered that the author does not only intend the exact form of the word that he has mentioned in the poem, but also the other derivates of that word.

For example, the word ظِلّ and other words made from its roots letters with the same meaning are mentioned 24 times in the *Qur'an* and its example is:

وَنُدْخِلُهُمْ ظِلًّا ظَلِيلًا – النساء

He ﷺ writes:

[52] .... وَكُلُّهَا (اي كُلُّ الظَّاءاتِ في القرآن) تَجِيْ

.... *All of them (i.e. the Zhas) come*

[53] فِي الظَّعْنِ ظِلِّ الظُّهْرِ عُظْمِ الْحِفْظ ... أَيْقِظْ وَ أَنْظُرْ عَظْمِ ظَهْرِ اللَّفْظ

In [the following words in the Qur'an] الظَّعْنِ, ظِلّ, الظُّهْرِ, عُظْمِ, الْحِفْظ, أيْقِظْ, أنْظُرْ, عَظْمِ, ظَهْرِ *and* اللَّفْظ ....

	Word	Number of occurrences in the Qur'an	Example
1	الظَّعْنِ	1	يَوْمَ ظَعْنِكُمْ – النحل
2	ظِلّ	24	وَنُدْخِلُهُمْ ظِلًّا ظَلِيْلًا – النساء
3	الظُّهْرِ	2	حِينَ تَضَعُونَ ثِيَابَكُمْ مِّنَ الظَّهِيرَةِ - النور
4	عُظْمِ	103	وَلَهُمْ عَذَابٌ عظِيمٌ – البقرة
5	الْحِفْظِ	42	حَافِظُواْ عَلَى الصَّلَوَاتِ - البقرة
6	أيْقِظْ	1	وَتَحْسَبُهُمْ أَيْقَاظاً وَهُمْ رُقُودٌ - الكهف
7	وَأَنْظُرْ	22	لَا يُخَفَّفُ عَنْهُمُ الْعَذَابُ وَلاَ هُمْ يُنْظَرُونَ – البقرة
8	عَظْمِ	15	وَانْظُرْ إِلَى العِظَامِ كَيْفَ نُنْشِزُهَا - البقرة
9	ظَهْرِ	16	وَرَآءَ ظُهُورِهِمْ كَأَنَّهُمْ لاَ يَعْلَمُونَ - البقرة
10	اللَّفْظِ	1	مَّا يَلْفِظُ مِن قَوْلٍ – ق

[54] ظَاهِرْ لَظَى شُوَاظُ كَظْمِ ظَلَمَا ... أُغْلُظْ ظَلاَمَ ظُفُرٍ انْتَظِرْ ظَمَا

[And also, in the following words] ظَلَمَا , كَظْمِ , شُوَاظُ , لَظَى , ظَاهِرْ
ظَمَا *and* انْتَظِرْ , ظُفُرٍ ,ظَلاَمَ , أُغْلُظْ ....

	Word	Number of occurrences in the Qur'an	Example
11	ظَاهِرْ	41	وَذَرُواْ ظَاهِرَ الإِثْمِ وَبَاطِنَهُ - الانعام
12	لَظَى	2	كَلاَّ إِنَّهَا لَظَى - المعارج
13	شُوَاظُ	1	يُرْسَلُ عَلَيْكُمَا شُوَاظٌ مِّن نَّارٍ وَنُحَاسٌ - الرحمن
14	كَظْمِ	6	وَالْكَاظِمِينَ الْغَيْظَ – آل عمران
15	ظَلَمَا	282	فَتَكُونَا مِنَ الْظَّالِمِينَ - البقرة
16	أُغْلُظْ	13	وَاغْلُظْ عَلَيْهِمْ - التحريم
17	ظَلاَمَ	26	وَتَرَكَهُمْ فِي ظُلُمَاتٍ لاَّ يُبْصِرُونَ - البقرة
18	ظُفُرٍ	1	وَعَلَى الَّذِينَ هَادُواْ حَرَّمْنَا كُلَّ ذِي ظُفُرٍ - الانعام
19	انْتَظِرْ	14	قُلِ انْتَظِرُوا إِنَّا مُنْتَظِرُونَ - الانعام
20	ظَمَا	3	لاَ يُصِيبُهُمْ ظَمَأٌ - التوبة

[55] أَظْفَرَ ظَنًّا كَيْفَ جَا[وَ] وَعْظٍ سِوَى ... عِضِينَ (اي ليس منه عِضِين بسورة الحجر) ..

[And also, in] أَظْفَرَ *and* ظَنًّا *however it comes, [and also in]* وَعْظٍ *except…*
.... عِضِينَ *[in Surah al-Hijr, here it's with a Dhad]…………..*

	Word	Number of occurrences in the Qur'an	Example
21	أَظْفَرَ	1	مِن بَعْدِ أَنْ أَظْفَرَكُمْ عَلَيْهِمْ - الفتح
22	ظَنًّا	69	ٱلَّذِينَ يَظُنُّونَ أَنَّهُم مُّلَٰقُواْ رَبِّهِمْ – البقرة
23	وَعْظ	25	وَمَوْعِظَةً لِّلْمُتَّقِينَ - البقرة

Note: the author highlights that in *Surah al-Hijr*, the word عِضِينَ is with a *Dhad* and not a *Zha*.

ٱلَّذِينَ جَعَلُوا الْقُرْآنَ عِضِينَ – الحجر (91)

Next the author indicates that the word ظَلَّ also has a *Zha* and then provides many examples of it from the *Qur'an*.

[55] .... ظَلَّ النَّحْلِ [وَ] زُخْرُفٍ سَوَا

And ظَلَّ *in Surah an-Nahl and Zukhruf is the same (i.e. the wording of the verse is the same in the two Surahs).*

[56] وَ ظَلْتَ ظَلْتُمْ وَ بِرُومٍ ظَلُّوا ... كَالْحِجْرِ ظَلَّتْ شُعَرَا [وَ] نَظَلّ

And [in] ظَلْتَ *,* ظَلْتُمْ *and* ظَلُّوا *in Surah Room,*

Just like in Surah al-Hijr [the same word is found]. [And in] ظَلَّتْ *and* نَظَلّ *of Surah Shu'ara*

[57] يَظْلَلْنَ ....

[And also, in] يَظْلَلْنَ

	Word	Number of occurrences in the Qur'an	Example
24	ظَلَّ	9	ظَلَّ وَجْهُهُ مُسْوَدّاً - النحل
24a	ظَلْتَ	These are examples of ظَلَّ	الَّذِي ظَلْتَ عَلَيْهِ عَاكِفاً - طه
24b	ظَلْتُمْ		فَظَلْتُمْ تَفَكَّهُونَ — الواقعة
24c	ظَلُّوا		لَّظَلُّواْ مِن بَعْدِهِ يَكْفُرُونَ — الروم فَظَلُّواْ فِيهِ يَعْرُجُونَ - الحجر
24d	ظَلَّتْ		فَظَلَّتْ أَعْنَاقُهُمْ — الشعراء
24e	نَظَلُّ		فَنَظَلُّ لَهَا عَاكِفِينَ — الشعراء
24f	يَظْلَلْنَ		فَيَظْلَلْنَ رَوَاكِدَ عَلَىٰ ظَهْرِهِ — الشورى

[57] .... مَحْظُورًا مَعَ الْمُحْتَظِرِ ... وَ كُنْتَ فَظًّا وَّجَمِيعِ النَّظَر

And [Zha is also found in] مَحْظُورًا *along with* الْمُحْتَظِر

And كُنْتَ فَظًّا *and all [words stemming from]* النَّظَر

	Word	Number of occurrences in the Qur'an	Example
25	مَحْظُورًا	1	وَمَا كَانَ عَطَآءُ رَبِّكَ مَحْظُوراً - الاسراء
26	الْمُحْتَظِرِ	1	فَكَانُواْ كَهَشِيمِ الْمُحْتَظِرِ - القمر
27	فَظًّا	1	وَلَوْ كُنْتَ فَظّاً غَلِيظَ الْقَلْبِ لَانْفَضُّوا مِنْ حَوْلِكَ — آل عمران
28	النَّظَرِ	86	وَ أَنْتُمْ تَنْظُرُونَ - البقرة

In line 58, the author makes the reader aware of three places in the *Qur'an*, where the letter is *Dhad* and not a *Zha.*

Those places are:

تَعۡرِفُ فِيۡ وُجُوۡهِهِمۡ نَضۡرَةَ النَّعِيۡمِ – المطففين (24)

وَ لَقّٰهُمۡ نَضۡرَةً وَّ سُرُوۡرًا – الانسان (11)

وُجُوۡهٌ يَّوۡمَئِذٍ نَّاضِرَةٌ ○ اِلٰى رَبِّهَا نَاظِرَةٌ – القيامة (22,23)

The author writes:

[58] إِلَّا بِوَيْلٍ (اي وَيْلٌ لِلْمُطَفِّفِين) [وَ] هَلْ (اي هَلْ أَتَى عَلى الْاِنْسَانِ) وَأُوْلَى نَاضِرَهْ (اي الأُولى في سورة القيامة) ... .

Except in Surah Al-Mutaffifeen, al-Insaan [the letter is Dhad and not a Zha] and [in al-Qiyaamah] the first one is نَاضِرَة *[and not* نَاظِرَة*]*

[58] .... وَ[جَمِيْعُ مَوَادِ] الْغَيْظِ [بالظاء] لَا الرَّعْدِ وَهُوْدٍ [فإِنَّ ضَادَهُما] قَاصِرَهْ [لأنها تُكْتَبُ بغير الالف]

And [all derivatives of] الْغَيْظِ *[have a Zha], but not the one in Surah Ra'd and Hud, [because it is a Dhad in those two Surahs, which is] short [compared to the Zha]*

	Word	Number of occurrences in the Qur'an	Example
29	الْغَيْظِ	11	قُلْ مُوتُوا بِغَيْظِكُمْ – آل عمران

Surah Ra'd and *Hud* contain a word that looks similar to غَيْظ , except that it has the letter *Dhad* instead of *Zha*. So, the author wants the reader to be careful, when reciting and not confuse the two words together.

وَ غِيضَ الْمَاءُ وَقُضِيَ الْأَمْرُ – هود (44)

وَمَا تَغِيضُ الْأَرْحَامُ – الرعد (8)

[59] وَ[جَمِيعُ مَوَادِ] الْحَظِّ لَا الْحَضِّ عَلَى الطَّعَامِ ... وَفِي ضَنِيْنٍ الْخِلَافُ سَامِيْ

And [all of the derivatives of] الْحَظِّ *[have a Zha], but not* الْحَضّ عَلَى الطَّعَام *[or its derivatives] ...*
And in [the word] ضَنِيْنٍ *there is sublime difference.*

	Word	Number of occurrences in the Qur'an	Example
30	الْحَظُّ	7	يُرِيدُ اللَّهُ أَلَّا يَجْعَلَ لَهُمْ حَظًّا فِي الآخِرَةِ – آل عمران
31	ضَنِيْنٍ	1	وَمَا هُوَ عَلَى الْغَيْبِ بِضَنِينٍ - التكوير *Ibn Kathir, Abu 'Amr* and *Kassai'* read it with a *Zha*, and the rest read it with a *Dhad*.

The derivatives of الْحَضّ are found in the *Qur'an* with a *Dhad* and not a *Zha*, and they come next to the words عَلَى الطَّعَام for example:

وَ لَا يَحُضُّ عَلَى طَعَامِ الْمِسْكِيْنِ – الماعون (3)

Did you know

It was narrated from *'Abdur-Rahman bin Abi Laila* that his father *Abu Laila* said:

I was sitting with the Prophet ﷺ when a bedouin came to him and said: 'I have a brother who is sick.' He ﷺ asked: 'What is the matter with your brother?' the bedouin said: 'He suffers from a slight mental instability.' He ﷺ said: 'Go and bring him.' So, the bedouin went and brought him.

He ﷺ made him sit down in front of him and I heard him seeking refuge for him with *Surah Fatihah*; four verses from the beginning of *Al-Baqarah*, two verses from its middle: (وَإِلَٰهُكُمْ إِلَٰهٌ وَاحِدٌ) *'And your God is one God'* and *Ayat Al-Kursi*; and three verses from its end; a verse from *Aal 'Imran*, I think it was: (شَهِدَ اللَّهُ أَنَّهُ لَا إِلَٰهَ إِلَّا هُوَ) *'Allah bears witness that none has the right to be worshipped but He,'* a verse from *Al-A'raf*: (إِنَّ رَبَّكُمُ اللَّهُ الَّذِي خَلَقَ) *'Indeed, your Lord is Allah,'* a verse from *Al-Mu'minun*: (وَمَنْ يَدْعُ مَعَ اللَّهِ إِلَٰهًا آخَرَ لَا بُرْهَانَ لَهُ بِهِ) *'And whoever worships besides Allah, any other god, of whom he has no proof,'* a verse from *Al-Jinn*: (وَأَنَّهُ تَعَالَىٰ جَدُّ رَبِّنَا مَا اتَّخَذَ صَاحِبَةً وَلَا وَلَدًا) *'And He, exalted is the Majesty of our Lord,'* ten verses from the beginning of *As-Safat*; three verses from the end of *Al-Hashr*; then (قُلْ هُوَ اللَّهُ أَحَدٌ) *'Say: He is Allah, the One,'* and *Al-Mu'awwidhatain* (*Surah Falaq* and *Nas*).

Then the Bedouin stood up, healed, and there was nothing wrong with him.

(*Sunan Ibn Majah*)

باب التحذيرات

Advices

[60] وَإِنْ تَلَاقَيَا الْبَيَانُ لَازِمٌ ... أَنْقَضَ ظَهْرَكَ يَعَضُّ الظَّالِمْ

[61] وَ اضْطُرَّ مَعْ وَعَظْتَ مَعْ أَفَضْتُمْ ... وَ صَفِّ هَا جِبَاهُهُم عَلَيْهِمْ

If *Dhad* (ض), *Zha* (ظ), *Ta* (ت), *Ta* (ط) appear next to each other, then the reciter needs to be extra cautious and pronounce them from their *Makhraj* with clarity and all of their *Sifaat*.

[60] وَإِنْ تَلَاقَيَا (اي الضادُ مع الظاء) الْبَيَانُ لَازِمُ ... أَنْقَضَ ظَهْرَكَ يَعَضُّ الظَّالِمُ

If both [the Dhad and Zha] meet, then clarity is necessary
[For example] أَنْقَضَ ظَهْرَكَ *and* يَعَضُّ الظَّالِمُ

[61] وَ [ايضا يَجِبُ بيانُ الضادِ من الطاء في] اضْطُرَّ مَعْ [بيانِ الظاء من التاء في]
وَعَظْتَ مَعْ [بيانِ الضادِ من التاء في] أَفَضْتُمُ ... وَ صَفِّ هَا جِبَاهُهُم عَلَيْهِمُ

And [it is necessary to distinguish the Dhad from the Ta in] اضْطُرَّ, *[the Zha from the Ta in]* وَعَظْتَ *along with [the Dhad from the Ta in]* أَفَضْتُمُ
And clarify the Ha in جِبَاهُهُم *[and]* عَلَيْهِم

يَعَضُّ الظَّالِمُ	These are examples of when a *Dhad* appears next to a *Zha*. The difficulty in this word is due to both letters being full mouth. So, extra caution must be taken to pronounce them clearly.
أَنْقَضَ ظَهْرَكَ	
اضْطُرَّ	This is an example of a *Dhad* next to a *Ta*. The common mistake here is to do *Idgham*.
وَعَظْتَ	In this example of *'Ain* next to *Zha*, the common mistake is to recite the *Zha* with an empty mouth. This mistake is easy to make because an empty mouth letter follows the *Zha*.
أَفَضْتُمُ	This is an example of a *Dhad* next to a *Ta*. The common mistake here is to do *Idgham*.
جِبَاهُهُم	Since the letter *Ha* is very weak and light, it is often undetected in pronunciation. So, the author stresses that the *Qari* should seek to pronounce it clearly.
عَلَيْهِم	

باب النون والميم المشددتين والميم الساكنة

Nun and *Mim Mushaddadatayn* and *Mim Sakinah*

[62] وَ أَظْهِرِ الْغُنَّةَ مِنْ نُونٍ وَّمِنْ ... مِيمٍ إِذَا مَا شُدِّدَا وَأَخْفِيَنْ

[63] الْمِيْمَ إِنْ تَسْكُنْ بِغُنَّةٍ لَّدى ... بَاءٍ عَلَى الْمُخْتَارِ مِنْ أَهْلِ الْأَدَا

[64] وَأَظْهِرَنْهَا عِنْدَ بَاقِي الْأَحْرُف ... وَاحْذَرْ لَدى وَاوٍ وَّ فَا أَنْ تَخْتَفِي

GHUNNAH

The *Makhraj* of the *Ghunnah* is the *Khayshum* and it is a permanent *Sifah* found inside *Mim* and *Nun*. However, its length and clarity differ depending upon the situation.

أنها في الساكن اكمل من المتحرك The *Ghunnah* in a *Sakin Mim* or *Nun* is more complete than in a *Mutaharrik Mim* or *Nun*.	compare نَعْبُدُ – اِنْ
و في المخفي أزيد من المظهر The *Ghunnah* in a *Mim* or *Nun* with *Ikhfaa* is longer than in a *Mim* or *Nun* with *Izhaar*.	compare مَنْ ءَامَنَ – يَنْزِلُ
و في المدغم أوفى من المخفي The *Ghunnah* in a *Mim* or *Nun* with *Idgham* is more complete than a *Mim* or *Nun* with *Ikhfaa*. In this scenario although the length of *Ghunnah* is the same in the two words, but it is clearer with *Idgham* than *Ikhfaa*. For the reason that in *Ikhfaa* not all of the air passes through the *Khayshum*, some of the air comes out of the mouth, making the *Ghunnah* weak.	compare يَنْزِلُ – اِنَّا

Since the *Ghunnah* is most pronounced when it is *Mushaddad*, the author says:

[62] وأَظْهِرِ الغُنَّةَ مِنْ نُونٍ وَمِنْ ... مِيمٍ إِذَا مَا شُدِّدَا ......

And make the Ghunnah clear in the Nun and in...
...the Mim, when they are Mushaddadah.

IKHFAA SHAFAWIY

If the *Mim* appears *Sakinah* and before a *Ba*, then it is recited with *Ikhfaa* and *Ghunnah*. *Ikhfaa* on the *Mim* is done by not closing the lips fully and allowing a small amount of air to pass between them. This will cause the *Mim* to become unclear. For example:

فَاحْكُمْ بَيْنَهُمْ – وَ مَن يَعْتَصِمْ بِاللهِ

Ibn al-Jazari, ﷺ describes *Ikhfaa Shafawiy* in line 62 and 63:

[62] .... وَأَخْفِيَنْ

And definitely hide (i.e. make unclear) ...

[63] الْمِيمَ إِنْ تَسْكُنْ بِغُنَّةٍ لَّدَى ... بَاءٍ عَلَى الْمُخْتَارِ مِنْ أَهْلِ الْأَدَا

...the Mim with Ghunnah, if it is Sakinah [and] next to ...
... the Ba according to the chosen opinion by the scholars of [perfect] pronunciation

IZHAAR SHAFAWIY

If a *Mim Sakinah* appears before any of the remaining letters of the Arabic alphabet after taking out *Ba* and *Mim*, then the *Mim* will be recited with *Izhaar*, i.e. short and clear. For example:

اَنْعَمْتَ

The author ﷺ cautions the reader of this mistake in line 64:

[64] وَأَظْهِرَنْهَا عِنْدَ بَاقِي الأَحْرُفِ ... .

And make it clear next to the remaining letters

A reciter must be cautious not to do *Idgham* or *Ikhfaa*, when the *Mim* appears before a *Waw* or a *Fa*. This is an easy mistake to make, since all three letters are pronounced from the lips.

The author ﷺ says:

[64] .... وَاحْذَرْ لَدَى وَاوٍ وَّ فَا أَنْ تَخْتَفِيْ

And be careful next to the Waw and Fa [not] to hide it

IDGHAM AL-MITHLAYN AS-SAGHIR

If a *Mim Sakinah* appears before another *Mim*, then *Idgham* is done. This is known as *Idgham al-Mithlayn as-Saghir*. For example:

وَ مَا لَهُمْ مِّنْ

Important Quranic Supplications

1

رَبَّنَآ اٰتِنَا فِي الدُّنْيَا حَسَنَةً وَّفِي الْاٰخِرَةِ حَسَنَةً وَّقِنَا عَذَابَ النَّارِ

Our Lord! Give us that which is good in this world and that which is good in the Hereafter, and save us from the torment of the Fire!

2

رَبَّنَا لَا تُزِغْ قُلُوْبَنَا بَعْدَ اِذْ هَدَيْتَنَا وَهَبْ لَنَا مِنْ لَّدُنْكَ رَحْمَةً اِنَّكَ اَنْتَ الْوَهَّابُ

Our Lord! Let not our hearts deviate [from the truth] after you have guided us and grant us your mercy. Truly, you are the bestower.

3

رَبَّنَآ اِنَّنَآ اٰمَنَّا فَاغْفِرْ لَنَا ذُنُوْبَنَا وَقِنَا عَذَابَ النَّارِ

Our Lord! We have indeed believed. So, forgive us our sins and save us from the punishment of the fire.

4

رَبَّنَا آمَنَّا بِمَا أَنْزَلْتَ وَاتَّبَعْنَا الرَّسُوْلَ فَاكْتُبْنَا مَعَ الشَّاهِدِيْنَ

Our Lord! We believe in what you have revealed and we follow the Messenger. Then write us down among those who bear witness.

5

رَبَّنَا تَقَبَّلْ مِنَّا إِنَّكَ أَنْتَ السَّمِيْعُ الْعَلِيْمُ

Our Lord! Accept [this] from us, for you are the all-hearing, the all-knowing.

باب أحكام النون الساكنة والتنوين

Nun Sakinah and *Tanween*

[65] وَحُكْمُ تَنْوِيْنٍ وَّ نُونٍ يُّلْفَى ... إِظْهَارٌ ادْغَامٌ وَّقَلْبٌ اِخْفَا

[66] فَعِنْدَ حَرْفِ الْحَلْقِ أَظْهِرْ وَادَّغِمْ ... فِي اللَّامِ وَالرَّا لَا بِغُنَّةٍ لَّزِمْ

[67] وَأَدْغِمَنْ بِغُنَّةٍ فِي يُومِنُ ... إِلَّا بِكِلْمَةٍ كَدُنْيَا عَنْوَنُوا

[68] وَالْقَلْبُ عِنْدَ الْبَا بِغُنَّةٍ كَذَا ... الِاخْفَا لَدَى بَاقِي الْحُرُوفِ أُخِذَا

There are four rules for *Nun Sakinah* and *Tanween*:

1. *Izhaar*
2. *Idgham*
3. *Qalb (Iqlaab)*
4. *Ikhfaa*

The author, *Ibn al-Jazari*, ﷺ says:

[65] وَحُكْمُ تَنْوِيْنٍ وَنُونٍ يُلْفَى ... إِظْهَارٌ ادْغَامٌ وَقَلْبٌ اخْفَا

And the rule[s] of Tanween and Nun, when they come with other words, are Izhaar, Idgham, Qalb and Ikhfaa

IZHAAR

If *Nun Sakinah* or *Tanween* appears before any of the throat letters, then the *Nun Sakinah* or *Tanween* is recited short and clear, without *Ghunnah*. The letters of the throat are:

Letters	Example
ء ه ع ح غ خ	مَنْ ءَامَنَ

The author ﷺ mentions this rule in line 66:

[66] فَعِنْدَ حَرْفِ الحَلْقِ أَظْهِرْ...... ... .

So, next to a throat letter, do Izhaar...

IDGHAM

If *Nun Sakinah* or *Tanween* appears before any of the *Yarmaloon* letters, then the *Nun Sakinah* or *Tanween* is merged into the *Yarmaloon* letter. The *Yarmaloon* letters are:

Letters	Example
يرملون = ي ر م ل و ن	مِنْ رَّبِّهِمْ

Idgham has two types:

1. *Idgham* without *Ghunnah*
2. *Idgham* with *Ghunnah*

Idgham without *Ghunnah* occurs when the *Nun Sakinah* or *Tanween* precedes the letter *Laam* or *Ra* from the *Yarmaloon* letters. For example:

مِنْ رَّبِّهِمْ – هُدًى لِّلْمُتَّقِيْنَ

The author ﷺ describes it as follows:

[66] .... وَادَّغِمْ ... فِي اللاَّمِ وَالرَّا لاَ بِغُنَّةٍ لَزِمْ

.... And do Idgham
...In Laam and Ra without Ghunnah, it is necessary [and complete Idgham]

On the other hand, *Idgham* with *Ghunnah* occurs when the *Nun Sakinah* or *Tanween* appears before the remaining *Yarmaloon* letters, which are found in the following:

Letters	Example
يُومِنُ = ي و م ن	عَنْ مَّنْ

However, the condition for *Idgham* is that *Nun Sakinah* or *Tanween* and the *Yarmaloon* letter are in two separate words. If they are in the same word, then *Idgham* is not permissible. For example, *Idgham* is not permissible in the following words:

دُنْيَا – بُنْيَانٌ – قِنْوَانٌ - صِنْوَانٍ

The author ﷺ says:

[67] وَأَدْغِمَنْ بِغُنَّةٍ فِي يُومِنُ ... إِلاَّ بِكِلْمَةٍ كَدُنْيَا عَنْوَنُوا

And definitely do Idgham with Ghunnah in يُومِنُ *[letters]*
Except if it is in [one] word, like دُنْيَا *and* عَنْوَنُوا

IQLAAB

If *Nun Sakinah* or *Tanween* appears before the letter *Ba*, then *Iqlaab* is done by changing the *Nun Sakinah* or *Tanween* into a *Mim* and pronouncing it with *Ghunnah* and *Ikhfaa*. *Iqlaab* is normally depicted by a small *Mim* above the *Nun Sakinah*. For example:

أَنۢبِئْهُمْ – عَلِيمٌۢ بِذَاتِ الصُّدُورِ

The author ﷺ says:

[68] وَالقَلْبُ عِنْدَ البَا بِغُنَّةٍ ....

And Qalb next to the Ba with Ghunnah,

IKHFAA

If *Nun Sakinah* or *Tanween* appears before the remaining letters of the alphabet, then *Ikhfaa* is done by pronouncing the *Nun* unclear and with *Ghunnah*. *Ikhfaa* is done keeping a small gap in the *Makhraj* of the *Nun* and releasing a small amount of air through the mouth as well as the *Khayshum*.

The author ﷺ says:

[68] .... كَذَا ... الِاخْفَا لَدَى بَاقِي الْحُرُوفِ أُخِذَا

.... [and] likewise
Ikhfaa with the remaining letters is taken (i.e. performed)

باب المد

Madd

[69] وَالْمَدُّ لاَزِمٌ وَّ وَاجِبٌ أَتٰى ... وَجَائِزٌ وَّ هْوَ وَقَصْرٌ ثَبَتَا

[70] فَلاَزِمٌ إِنْ جَاءَ بَعْدَ حَرْفِ مَدْ ... سَاكِنُ حَالَيْنِ وَبِالطُّولِ يُمَدْ

[71] وَ وَاجِبٌ إِنْ جَاءَ قَبْلَ هَمْزَة ... مُتَّصِلًا إِنْ جُمِعَا بِكِلْمَة

[72] وَجَائِزٌ إِذَا أَتٰى مُنْفَصِلَا ... أَوْ عَرَضَ السُّكُونُ وَقْفًا مُّسْجَلَا

THE TRANSLATION

[69] وَالمَدُّ لاَزِمٌ وَوَاجِبٌ أَتَى ... وَجَائِزٌ وَهْوَ وَقَصْرٌ ثَبَتَا

And the Madd is Laazim, and it [also] comes as Waajib…
…as well as Jaaiz, in which it (i.e. extending) and shortening are both valid

[70] فَلاَزِمٌ إِنْ جَاءَ بَعْدَ حَرْفِ مَدْ ... سَاكِنُ حَالَيْنِ وَبِالطُّولِ يُمَدْ

So, it will be necessary, if after a Madd letter, appears…
… a Sakin letter, [whose Sukun is necessary] in both states [of Wasl and Waqf]. It [should be] lengthened to 3 Alif lengths

[71] وَوَاجِبٌ إِنْ جَاءَ قَبْلَ هَمْزَةِ ... مُتَّصِلًا إِنْ جُمِعَا بِكِلْمَةِ

And it is mandatory, if it comes before a Hamzah…
…joint, [in other words] if they both gather in one word.

[72] وَجَائِزٌ إِذَا أَتَى مُنْفَصِلَا ... أَوْ عَرَضَ السُّكُونُ وَقْفًا مُسْجَلَا

And it will be permissible, if it comes separately
Or if the Sukun is temporary, generally due to Waqf

The author, *Ibn al-Jazari,* ﷺ divides the *Mudud* into three main types. Please see the diagram on the next page for a better understanding of them.

المدود

واجب

If there is a *Hamzah* after the *Madd* letter in the same word, then it is called:

المد المتصل

For example:

جَآء

Length:

<u>6 *Harakaat*</u> (according to *Imam Warsh* & *Hamzah*)

<u>4 *Harakaat*</u> (according to the rest)

لازم

If after the *Madd* letter there is a Permanent *Sukun*, then it is called:

المد اللازم

For example:

كَآفَّةً (كَافْفَةً)

Length:

<u>6 *Harakaat*</u> (3 *Alifs*)

جائز

First: If there is a *Hamzah* after the *Madd* letter in a separate word, then it is called:

المد المنفصل

For example:

فِيْٓ أَنْفُسِهِمْ

Length:

<u>6 *Harakaat*</u> (according to *Imam Warsh* & *Hamzah*)

<u>4 *Harakaat*</u> (according to *Imam ibn Amir, 'Asim, al-Kassa'i,* & *Khalf*)

<u>2 or 4 *Harakaat*</u> (according to *Imam Qalun* & *al-Duri*)

Second: If after the *Madd* letter there is a temporary *Sukun* due to *Waqf*, then it is called:

المد العارض للسكون

For example:

تَعْلَمُونَ

Length:

<u>2, 4 or 6 *Harakaat*</u>

Note: The length of each *Madd* is based upon what is mentioned in *Ibn Yalushah's* commentary:

الفوائد المفهمة في شرح الجزرية المقدمة

للامام ابو عبد الله فخر الدين محمد بن على بن يوسف بن يالوشه المكي الاندلسي اصلا رحمه الله

INTRODUCTION INTO THE NEXT SECTION

The next section is about the correct and incorrect manner of stopping recitation (*Waqf*). It is helpful to understand how the types of stops are divided, prior to studying the next section. When a person stops recitation, the verse is divided into two parts:

1. The portion of the verse that is before the *Waqf*
2. The portion of the verse which is after the *Waqf*.

Imagine the following line is a verse with a *Waqf* in between, splitting the verse into two parts:

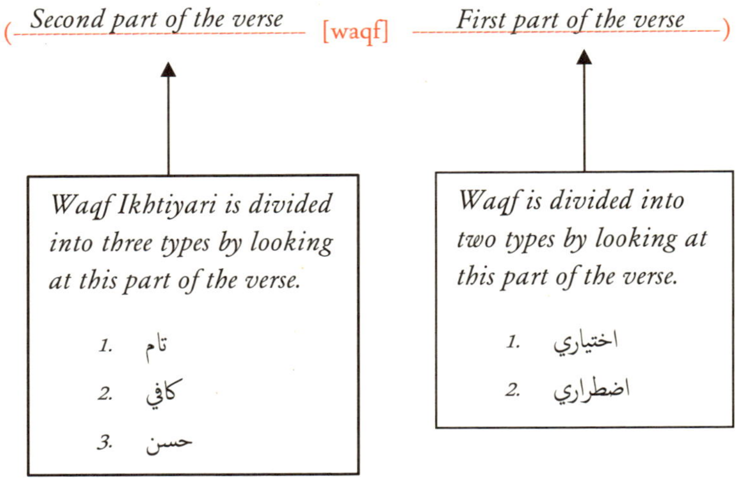

باب معرفة الوقف والابتداء
Knowing where to stop and start

[73] وَ بَعْدَ تَجْوِيْدِكَ لِلْحُرُوف ... لَا بُدَّ مِنْ مَّعْرِفَةِ الْوُقُوف

[74] وَ الِابْتِدَاءِ وَهْيَ تُقْسَمُ إِذَنْ ... ثَلاَثَةً تَامٌ وَّكَافٍ وَّحَسَنْ

[75] وَهْيَ لِمَا تَمَّ فَإِنْ لَّمْ يُوجَد ... تَعَلُّقٌ أَوْ كَانَ مَعْنًى فَابْتَدِيْ

[76] فَالتَّامُ فَالْكَافِي وَ لَفْظًا فَامْنَعَنْ ... إِلَّا رُؤُوسَ الْآيِ جَوِّزْ فَالْحَسَنْ

[77] وَغَيْرُ مَا تَمَّ قَبِيحٌ وَّلَهُ ... اَلْوَقْفُ مُضْطَرًّا وَيُبْدَا قَبْلَهُ

[78] وَلَيْسَ فِي الْقُرْآنِ مِنْ وَّقْفٍ وَّجَبْ ... وَلاَ حَرَامٌ غَيْرَ مَا لَهُ سَبَبْ

Imam Ibn al-Jazari ﷺ writes in his book, *'Al-Nashr fi al-Qira'aat al-'Ashr'*:

أنَّ الوقفَ يَنقَسِمُ إلى اختياريّ وَ اضطراريّ لأنَّ الكلامَ إمَّا أن يَتِمَّ أو لَا، فَإنْ تَمَّ كَانَ اختيارياً

(*Interpretation*) *Waqf* has two types, depending upon if the sentence is complete or incomplete with regards to the grammar and meaning:

1. *Ikhtiyari*
2. *Idhtirari.*

If the sentence is complete upon stopping, then the *Waqf* is called *Ikhtiyari* and if it is incomplete, it is called *Idhtirari.*

الوقف

الوقف الاختياري

The meaning and grammar of what has been recited is complete, i.e. it is a complete sentence. For example:

اَلْحَمْدُ لله – *All praise are for Allah*

الوقف الاضطراري

The meaning and grammar of what has been recited is incomplete. For example:

اَلْحَمْدُ – *All praise ......*

وَكَوْنُهُ تامًّا لا يَخْلُوْ إمَّا أن لا يكونَ له تعلقٌ بما بعدَه البَتَّةَ أيْ لَا مِن جِهَةِ اللفظِ و لَا مِنْ جِهَةِ المعنى فهو الوقفُ الذي اصْطَلَحَ عليه الأئمَّةُ (بالتام) لِتَمَامِه المطلق، يُوقَفُ عليه ويُبْتَدَأُ بما بعدَه

(*Interpretation*) *Waqf Ikhtiyari* can be further divided by considering whether or not it has a connection to the sentence following it in meaning or grammar. If it does not have a connection to the next passage after the stop, neither in grammar and nor in meaning, then this is what the scholars call ***al-Waqf ut-Taam*** (the complete stop).

This type of *Waqf* is permissible and it is also permissible to start recitation from the next passage after the place of *Waqf*. See the following diagram:

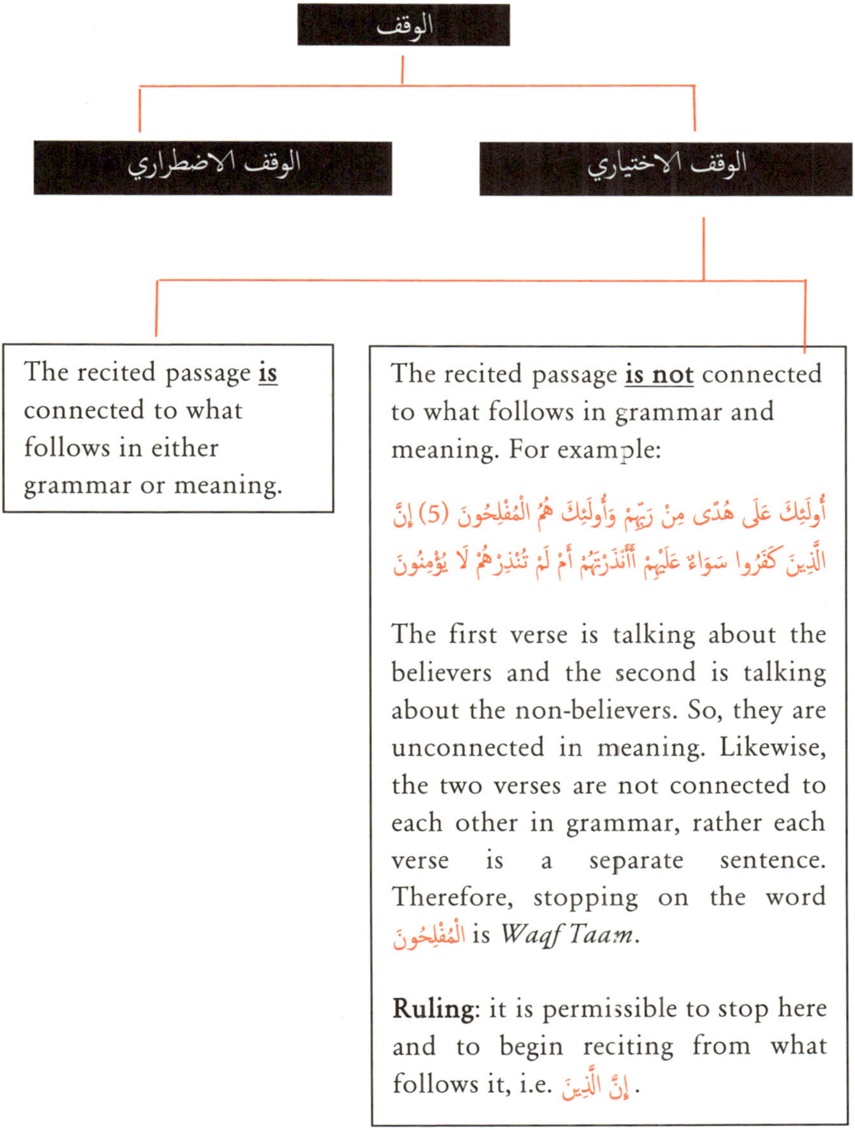

وَ إنْ كانَ له تعلقٌ فلا يَخْلُوْ هذا التعلقُ إمَّا أن يكون مِن جِهَةِ المعنى فقط وهو الوقفُ الْمُصْطَلَحُ عليه (بالكافي) للاكْتِفَاءِ به عما بعده. واسْتِغْنَاءِ ما بعده عنه وهو كالتام في جوازِ الوقفِ عليه والابتداءِ بما بعده وإن كان التعلقُ مِن جهةِ اللفظِ فهو الوقفُ المصطلحُ عليه (بالحسن) لأنه في نَفْسِه حَسَنٌ مُفِيْدٌ يَجُوْزُ الوقفُ عليه دونَ الابتداءِ بما بعده للتعلقِ اللفظيِّ إلا أن يكونَ رَأسَ آية ...

(*Interpretation*) If *Waqf* is done upon a sentence that is connected to what follows, then that *Waqf* has two types, depending upon if it is connected in meaning or grammar:

1. ***Al-Waqf ul-Kafi***
   This is the stop that is done after a sentence, which is connected to what follows in meaning but not in grammar. The ruling of this is the same as *al-Waqf ut-Taam*. For example:

   يُخَادِعُونَ اللَّهَ وَالَّذِينَ آمَنُوا وَمَا يَخْدَعُونَ إِلَّا أَنْفُسَهُمْ وَمَا يَشْعُرُونَ

   Stopping on the word آمَنُوا is *Al-Waqf ul-Kafi*, because the next sentence does not depend on the previous in grammar, but the topic is the same.

2. ***Al-Waqf ul-Hasan***
   This is the stop that is done after a sentence, but the next sentence is connected to it in grammar. For example:

   اَلْحَمْدُ لِلّٰهِ رَبِّ الْعَالَمِيْنَ

   Although اَلْحَمْدُ لِلّٰهِ is a complete sentence, but the text following it (رَبِّ الْعَالَمِيْنَ), depends on it in grammar, i.e. they are part of the same sentence. Therefore, stopping at اَلْحَمْدُ لِلّٰهِ is *al-Waqf ul-Hasan*.

   This is a permissible stop, but it is not permissible to begin recitation from what follows, unless it is the end of a verse.

Observe the diagram:

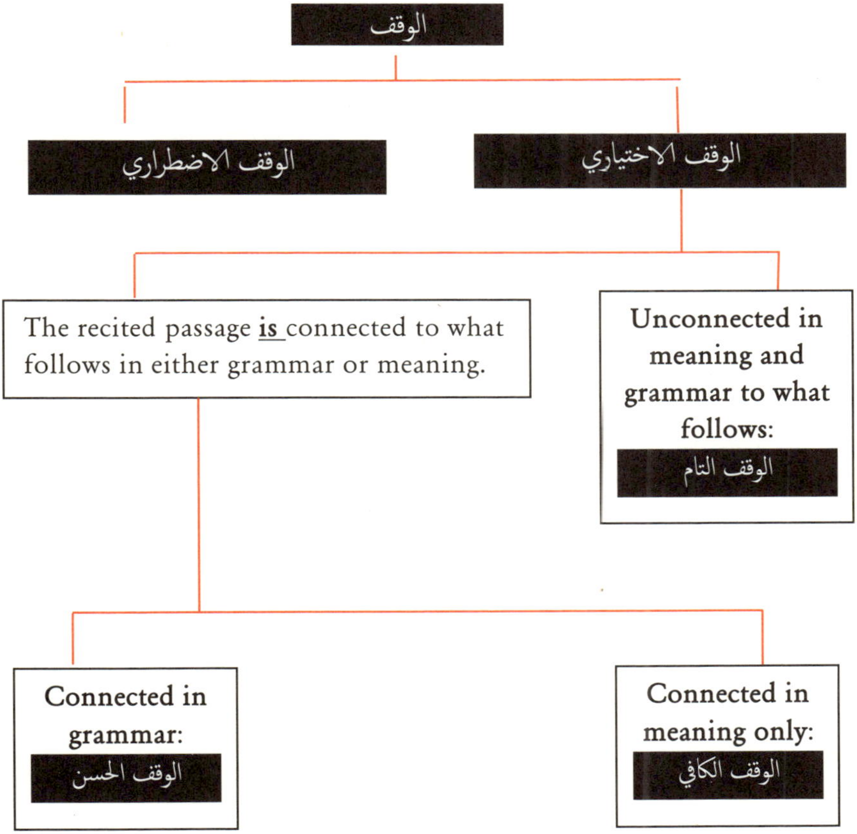

... وَ إن لَّم يَتِمَّ الكلامُ كَانَ الوقفُ عليه اضطرارياً وهو المصطلحُ عليه (بالقبيح) لا يَجُوْزُ تَعَمُّدُ الوقفِ عليه إلا لضرورةٍ مِن انْقِطَاعِ نَفَسٍ ونحوِه لعدمِ الفائدةِ أو لِفَسادِ المعنى.

If the sentence is incomplete when stopping, then that *Waqf* is *Idhtirari*, which is called ***Al-Waqf ul-Qabih***. It is not permissible to stop here unless there is a necessity, such as running out of breath, as stopping here has no benefit and it could lead to the meaning being distorted.

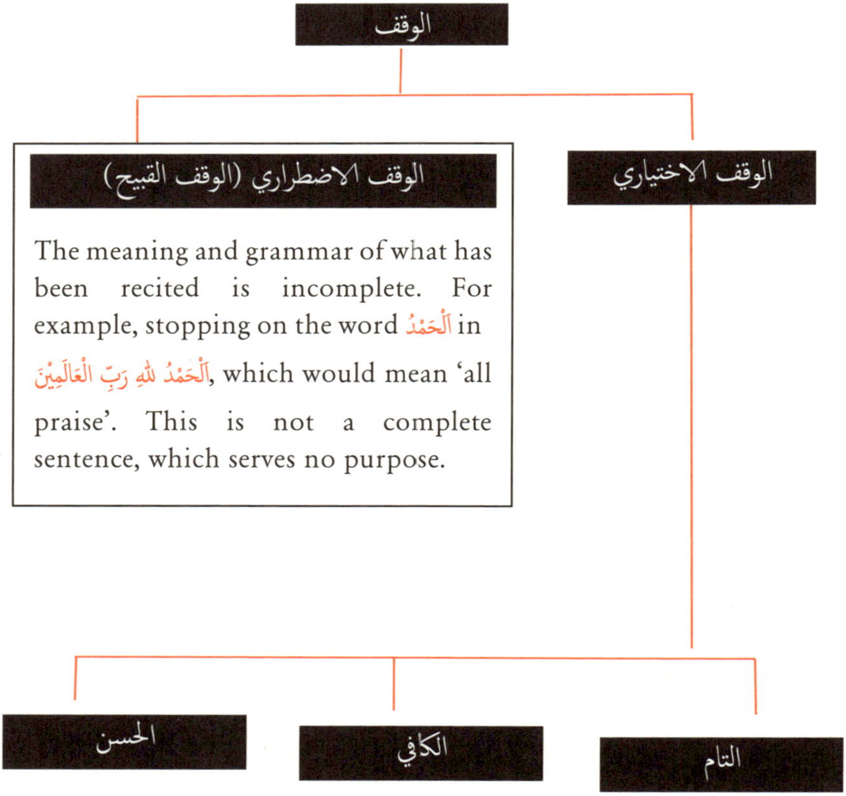

Understanding the types of *Waqf* from the poem:

The author ﷺ first divides the *Waqf Ikhtiyari* into three types:

[73] وَ بَعْدَ تَجْوِيْدِكَ لِلْحُرُوفِ ... لَا بُدَّ مِنْ مَعْرِفَةِ الْوُقُوفِ

And after you have [learnt] the Tajweed of Huruf,
It is necessary to know [where to] stop ...

[74] وَ الِابْتِدَاءِ وَهِيَ تُقْسَمْ إِذَنْ ... ثَلَاثَةٌ تَامٌ وَكَافٍ وَحَسَنْ

... and start. And it (i.e. Waqf) is thus divided
[into] three: Taam, Kaafi and Hasan

[75] وَهِيَ لِمَا تَمَّ ....

And this is when the [meaning and grammar] is complete [on stopping].

It is understood from the first few words in line 75, that these are types of *Waqf Ikhtiyari*.

WAQF TAAM

Concerning *Waqf Taam*, he says:

[75] .... فَإِنْ لَمْ يُوجَدِ ... تَعَلُّقٌ [بما بعدَه] .... فَ[قِف على ما تَمَّ وَ] ابْتَدِي

So, if there isn't a connection [to the next sentence], then [stop upon what
has been recited and then] begin [recitation from that point]

[76] فَ [سَمِّهِ] التَّامَ.......... ... .

And [called it] Taam.

WAQF KAAFI

Concerning *Waqf Kaafi*, he says:

[75] .... أَوْ كَانَ [فيه تعلقٌ لما بعده] مَعْنًى فَ[قِف على ما تَمَّ وَ] ابْتَدِي

Or [if there is a connection to what follows in] meaning [only], then [stop
upon what has been recited and then] begin [recitation from that point]

[76] ...... فَ [سَمِّهِ] الْكَافِي............ ... .

And [called it] Kaafi.

WAQF HASAN

Concerning *Waqf Hasan*, he says:

[76] وَ[لَوْ كَانَ فِيْهِ تَعَلُّقٌ لما بعده] لَفْظًا فَامْنَعَنْ [الابتداءَ بِمَا بَعدَه] ...
إِلاَّ رُؤُوسَ الآيِ جَوِّزْ فَ [وَقْفُهُ] الْحَسَنْ

And [if there is a connection to what follows] in words (i.e. grammatically), then you are Prohibited [to start recitation with what follows],
Except at the start of verses it is permissible and [this Waqf is] Hasan.

WAQF QABIH (*IDHTIRARI*)

The author, *Ibn al-Jazari*, ﷺ says:

[77] وَغَيْرُ مَا تَمَّ قَبِيحٌ وَ [يَجُوْزُ] لَهُ ... الْوَقْفُ مُضْطَرًّا وَيُبْدَا قَبْلَهُ

And if the [meaning and grammar] is not complete, then it is a foul [Waqf]. And it is [permissible] for him…
… to stop [only] when compelled, and start [from a point] before it

Finally, the author mentions that, there isn't a *Waqf* in the *Qur'an* that is necessary, missing which would be a sin, unless there are is a reason that makes it necessary. Likewise, there isn't a *Waqf* in the *Qur'an* that is *Haram*, unless there is a reason for it to be *Haram*.

For example, if someone intended to stop recitation on the words وَمَا مِنْ إِلٰهٍ *(And there is no deity)* in the verse إِنَّ هَـٰذَا لَهُوَ الْقَصَصُ الْحَقُّ ۚ وَمَا مِنْ إِلٰهٍ إِلَّا اللهُ *(Indeed, this is the true narration. And there is no deity except Allah)*, that would alter the meaning of the *Qur'an*. Stopping here deliberately is *Haram*. The author says:

[78] وَلَيْسَ فِي الْقُرْآنِ مِنْ وَقْفٍ وَجَبْ ... وَلاَ حَرَامٌ غَيْرَ مَا لَهُ سَبَبْ

And there isn't a necessary stop in the Qur'an
And nor a prohibited [stop], except for that which has a reason

باب المقطوع والموصول

Detached and Attached Words

[79] وَاعْرِفْ لِمَقْطُوعٍ وَمَوْصُولٍ وَتَا ... فِي مُصْحَفِ الْإِمَامِ فِيمَا قَدْ أَتَى

[80] فَاقْطَعْ بِعَشْرِ كَلِمَاتٍ أَنْ لَا ... مَعْ مَلْجَأً وَلَا إِلَهَ إِلَّا

[81] وَ تَعْبُدُوا يَاسِينَ ثَانِي هُودَ لَا ... يُشْرِكْنَ تُشْرِكْ يَدْخُلَنْ تَعْلُوا عَلَى

[82] أَنْ لَا يَقُولُوا لَا أَقُولَ إِنْ مَا ... بِالرَّعْدِ وَ الْمَفْتُوحَ صِلْ وَعَنْ مَا

[83] نُهُوا اقْطَعُوا مِنْ مَا بِرُومٍ وَالنِّسَا ... خُلْفُ الْمُنَافِقِينَ أَمْ مَنْ أَسَّسَا

[84] فُصِّلَتِ النِّسَا وَذِبْحٍ حَيْثُ مَا ... وَ أَنْ لَمِ الْمَفْتُوحَ كَسْرَ إِنَّ مَا

[85] الْأَنْعَامَ وَالْمَفْتُوحَ يَدْعُونَ مَعَا ... وَخُلْفُ الْأَنْفَالِ وَنَحْلٍ وَقَعَا

[86] وَكُلِّ مَا سَأَلْتُمُوهُ وَاخْتُلِفْ ... رُدُّوا كَذَا قُلْ بِئْسَمَا وَ الْوَصْلَ صِفْ

[87] خَلَفْتُمُونِي وَ اشْتَرَوْا فِي مَا اقْطَعَا ... أُوحِيَ أَفَضْتُمُ اشْتَهَتْ يَبْلُوا مَعَا

[88] ثَانِي فَعَلْنَ وَقَعَتْ رُومٍ كِلَا ... تَنْزِيلِ شُعَرَا وَغَيْرَهَا صِلَا

[89] فَأَيْنَمَا كَالنَّحْلِ صِلْ وَمُخْتَلِفْ ... فِي الشُّعَرَا الْأَحْزَابِ وَالنِّسَا وُصِفْ

[90] وَصِلْ فَإِلَّمْ هُودَ أَلَّنْ نَجْعَلَا ... نَجْمَعَ كَيْلَا تَحْزَنُوا تَأْسَوْا عَلَى

[91] حَجٌّ عَلَيْكَ حَرَجٌ وَقَطْعُهُمْ ... عَنْ مَنْ يَشَاءُ مَنْ تَوَلَّى يَوْمَ هُمْ

[92] وَ مَالِ هَذَا وَ الَّذِينَ هَؤُلَا ... تَحِينَ فِي الْإِمَامِ صِلْ وَوُهِّلَا

[93] وَ وَزَنُوهُمُ وَ كَالُوهُمُ صِلِ

كَذَا مِنَ الْ وَ يَا وَ هَا لَا تَفْصِلِ

The author says:

[79] وَاعْرِفْ لِمَقْطُوعٍ وَمَوْصُولٍ وَتَا ... فِي مُصْحَفِ الإِمَامِ فِيمَا قَدْ أَتَى

And learn the detached and attached [words] as well as the feminine Taa
In the Mushaf of the Imam from that which follows

In certain places in the *Masahif* of *Sayyiduna Uthman*, some words are connected to others in writing, whilst in other places the same two words are written separately. It is important to know the script of the *Qur'an*, as that helps in knowing where and how to stop.

أَنْ لَّا

The words أَنْ لَّا are separated in 10 places in the *Mushaf*, even though *Idgham* is done in pronunciation. Those 10 places are:

[80] فَاقْطَعْ بِعَشْرِ كَلِمَاتٍ أَنْ لَا ... مَعْ مَلْجَأ وَ لَا إِلَهَ إِلَّا

وَ ظَنُّوٓا اَنْ لَّا مَلْجَاَ مِنَ اللهِ اِلَّآ اِلَيْهِ – التوبة (117)

وَ اَنْ لَّآ اِلٰهَ اِلَّا هُوَ – هود (14)

[81] وَ تَعْبُدُوا يَاسِينَ[وَ] ثَانِي هُودَ [وَ]لَا ... يُشْرِكْنَ[وَ] تُشْرِكْ[وَ] يَدْخُلَنْ [وَ] تَعْلُوا عَلَى

لَمْ اَعْهَدْ اِلَيْكُمْ يٰبَنِيٓ اٰدَمَ اَنْ لَّا تَعْبُدُوا الشَّيْطٰنَ– يس (60)

اَنْ لَّا تَعْبُدُوٓا اِلَّا اللهَ – هود (26)

عَلٰٓى اَنْ لَّا يُشْرِكْنَ بِاللهِ شَيْئًا – الممتحنة (12)

اَنْ لَّا تُشْرِكْ بِيْ شَيْئًا – الحج (26)

اَنْ لَّا يَدْخُلَنَّهَا الْيَوْمَ – القلم (24)

وَّ اَنْ لَّا تَعْلُوْا عَلَى اللهِ – الدخان (19)

[82] .[وَ] أَنْ لَا يَقُولُوا [وَ] لَا أَقُولَ ....

اَنْ لَّا يَقُوْلُوْا عَلَى اللهِ اِلَّا الْحَقَّ – الاعراف (169)

حَقِيقٌ عَلَىٰٓ اَنْ لَّآ اَقُوْلَ عَلَى اللهِ اِلَّا الْحَقَّ – الاعراف (105)

In all other places, *Idgham* of the *Nun* is done into the *Laam* in pronunciation and in writing. For example:

اَفَلَا يَرَوْنَ اَلَّا يَرْجِعُ اِلَيْهِمْ قَوْلًا – طه (89)

Note: There is a difference in the *Masahif* on the words أَنْ لَّا in *Surah AL-Anbiya'*. In some *Masahif*, *Idgham* is done in writing and in others they are written separately. *Ibn Jazari* does not mention this in his poem, as it is a basic text in *Tajweed*. However, *Mulla Ali al-Qari* and many other scholars have mentioned it in their commentaries. The verse is:

اَنْ لَّآ اِلٰهَ اِلَّآ اَنْتَ سُبْحٰنَكَ - الانبياء (87)

إِنْ مَا

All of the *Masahif* are united in keeping the words إِنْ مَا separated in verse 40 of *Surah Ra'd*. In all other places, the *Nun* is merged into the *Laam* in writing.

[82] .... [اقْطَعْ] إِنْ مَا ... بِالرَّعْدِ ....

وَ اِنْ مَّا نُرِيَنَّكَ بَعْضَ الَّذِىْ نَعِدُهُمْ – الرعد (40)

أَمَّا (أَمْ مَا)

All of the *Masahif* are united in merging the first *Mim* into the second in writing, for example:

[82] .... وَ[أَمَّا] الْمَفْتُوحَ [هَمْزَتُه] صِلْ ......

اَمَّا اشْتَمَلَتْ عَلَيْهِ اَرْحَامُ الْاُنْثَيَيْنِ – الانعام (143)

عَنْ مَا

All of the *Masahif* are the same in separating the *Nun* in writing from the *Mim* in verse 166 of *surah Al-A'raf.* In all other places *Idgham* is done in writing also.

[82] .... وَ [اِقْطَعْ فِي] عَنْ مَا

[83] نُهُوا................ ... .

فَلَمَّا عَتَوْا عَنْ مَّا نُهُوْا عَنْهُ – الاعراف (166)

مِنْ مَّا

All of the *Masahif* are the same in separating the *Nun* in writing from the *Mim* in 2 verses only.

[83] ..... اقْطَعُوا مِنْ مَا بِرُومٍ وَالنِّسَا ... .

هَلْ لَّكُمْ مِّنْ مَّا مَلَكَتْ اَيْمَانُكُمْ – الروم (28)

فَمِنْ مَّا مَلَكَتْ اَيْمَانُكُمْ – النساء (25)

However, in verse 10 of *Surah Munafiqun*, the *Masahif* are different. In some of them it is written separately, whilst in others it is joint.

[83] .... [ثَبَتَ] خُلْفُ [مَا فِي] الْمُنَافِقِينَ ....

وَ اَنْفِقُوْا مِنْ مَّا رَزَقْنٰكُمْ – المنافقون (10)

أَمْ مَنْ

All of the *Masahif* are the same in writing the first *Mim* separate from the second in 4 places only.

[83] ....[اِقْطَعْ فِي] أَمْ مَنْ أَسَّسَا

[84] .[وَ] فُصِّلَتْ [وَ] النِّسَا وَ ذِبْحٍ (اي الصافات) ....

اَمْ مَّنْ اَسَّسَ بُنْيَانَهٗ - التوبة (108)

اَمْ مَّنْ يَّأْتِيٓ اٰمِنًا يَّوْمَ الْقِيٰمَةِ – فصلت (41)

اَمْ مَّنْ يَّكُوْنُ عَلَيْهِمْ وَكِيْلًا – النساء (109)

فَاسْتَفْتِهِمْ اَهُمْ اَشَدُّ خَلْقًا اَمْ مَّنْ خَلَقْنَا – الصافات (11)

In all other verses it is written connected. For example:

اَمَّنْ خَلَقَ السَّمٰوٰتِ وَالْاَرْضَ – النمل (60)

حَيْثُ مَا

All of the *Masahif* are the same in writing the two words separate always. However, this combination only occurs in two verses of *Surah Baqarah*.

[84] ....[اِقْطَعْ] حَيْثُ مَا ... .

وَ حَيْثُ مَا كُنْتُمْ فَوَلُّوْا وُجُوْهَكُمْ شَطْرَهٗ - البقرة (144)

وَ حَيْثُ مَا كُنْتُمْ فَوَلُّوْا وُجُوْهَكُمْ شَطْرَهٗ ۙ لِئَلَّا – البقرة (150)

أَنْ لَمْ

Whenever this combination occurs in the *Qur'an*, according to all of the *Masahif,* they are written separately. Here are two examples of it:

[84] .... وَ [اِقْطَعْ] أَنْ لَم المَفْتُوحَ ....

ذٰلِكَ اَنْ لَّمْ يَكُنْ رَّبُّكَ مُهْلِكَ الْقُرٰى بِظُلْمٍ – الانعام (131)

اَيَحْسَبُ اَنْ لَّمْ يَرَهٗٓ اَحَدٌ – البلد (7)

اِنَّ مَا

According to all of the *Masahif,* the two words are written separately in verse 134 of *Surah al-An'aam*.

[84] .... [اِقْطَعْ] كَسْرَ إِنَّ مَا

[85] . [في] اَلانْعَامِ........ ... .

(اي إقْطَعْ إِنَّ المكسورة عن مَا الموصولةِ في الانعام)

اِنَّ مَا تُوْعَدُوْنَ لَاٰتٍ - الانعام (134)

أَنَّ مَا

The words أَنَّ مَا are written separately in two verses only, according to all *Masahif.*

[85] ... وَ [اِقْطَعْ أَنَّ] المَفْتُوحَ [هَمْزَتُه في] يَدْعُونَ مَعَا (اي يَدْعُونَ في الموضعين) ... .

وَ اَنَّ مَا يَدْعُوْنَ مِنْ دُوْنِهٖ هُوَ الْبَاطِلُ – الحج (62)

ذٰلِكَ بِاَنَّ اللّٰهَ هُوَ الْحَقُّ وَ اَنَّ مَا يَدْعُوْنَ مِنْ دُوْنِهِ الْبَاطِلُ – لقمان (30)

However, the *Masahif* differ in two other verses.

[85] .... وَخُلْفُ الانْفَالِ وَنَحْلٍ وَقَعَا

وَ اعْلَمُوٓا اَنَّمَا غَنِمْتُمْ مِّنْ شَيْءٍ – الانفال (41) - (أَنَّ مَا)

اِنَّمَا عِنْدَ اللهِ هُوَ خَيْرٌ لَّكُمْ – النحل (95) – (إِنَّ مَا)

كُلِّ مَا

According to all *Masahif*, the two words are written separately in verse 34 of *Surah Ibrahim*.

[86] وَ [اِقْطَعْ] كُلِّ مَا سَأَلْتُمُوهُ........ ... .

وَ اٰتٰكُمْ مِّنْ كُلِّ مَا سَاَلْتُمُوْهُ – ابراهيم (34)

However, there is a difference in the *Masahif* in 4 other verses. But the author only indicates to one of them, in order to keep his poem concise.

[86] .... وَاخْتُلِفْ [في] ... رُدُّوا [وَالاعراف وَ المؤمنون وَ الملك] .....

كُلَّمَا رُدُّوْٓا اِلَى الْفِتْنَةِ اُرْكِسُوْا فِيْهَا – النساء (91)

كُلَّمَا دَخَلَتْ اُمَّةٌ لَّعَنَتْ اُخْتَهَا – الاعراف (38)

كُلَّ مَا جَآءَ اُمَّةً رَّسُوْلُهَا كَذَّبُوْهُ – المؤمنون (44)

كُلَّمَآ اُلْقِيَ فِيْهَا فَوْجٌ – الملك (8)

In all other places it is written separately.

بِئْسَ مَا (بِئْسَمَا)

Similarly, the *Masahif* differ in the words بِئْسَ مَا in verse 93 *Surah Baqarah*.

[86] ....كَذَا [أُخْتُلِفَ فِي] قُلْ بِئْسَمَا ....

قُلْ بِئْسَمَا يَأْمُرُكُمْ بِهِۦٓ إِيمَانُكُمْ – البقرة (93)

In two verses the words بِئْسَ مَا are joint in all of the *Masahif*:

[86] .... وَ الْوَصْلَ صِفْ [فِي]

[87] خَلَفْتُمُونِي وَ اشْتَرَوْا....... ... .

قَالَ بِئْسَمَا خَلَفْتُمُونِى مِنۢ بَعْدِىٓ – الاعراف (150)

بِئْسَمَا اشْتَرَوْا بِهِۦٓ أَنفُسَهُمْ – البقرة (90)

In all other verses it is written separately in all of the *Masahif*.

فِي مَا

These two words are written separately in 11 verses of the *Qur'an* and in all other places they are joint.

[87] .... فِي مَا اقْطَعَا (اي اِقْطَعَنْ فِي مَا فِي اَحَدَ عشرةَ موضعًا) ...[الذي قبل] أُوحِيْ [وَ] أَفَضْتُمْ [وَ] اشْتَهَتْ [وَبعدَ] يَبْلُوا مَعَا (اي في الموضِعَينِ)

[88] . [وَ قبلَ] ثَانِي فَعَلْنَ [وَ] وَقَعَتْ (اي سورة الواقعة) [وَالذي في سورة] رُومٍ [وَ] كِلاَ ... تَنْزِيلِ (اي سورة الزمر) [وَ] شُعَرَا وَغَيْرَهَا صِلَا

قُلْ لَّآ أَجِدُ فِى مَآ أُوحِىَ إِلَىَّ مُحَرَّمًا – الانعام (145)

لَمَسَّكُمْ فِى مَآ أَفَضْتُمْ فِيهِ عَذَابٌ عَظِيمٌ – النور (14)

وَ هُمْ فِيْ مَا اشْتَهَتْ اَنْفُسُهُمْ خٰلِدُوْنَ – الانبياء (102)

وَّ لٰكِنْ لِّيَبْلُوَكُمْ فِيْ مَا اٰتٰكُمْ فَاسْتَبِقُوا الْخَيْرٰتِ – المائدة (48)

لِّيَبْلُوَكُمْ فِيْ مَا اٰتٰكُمْ – الانعام (165)

فَلَا جُنَاحَ عَلَيْكُمْ فِيْ مَا فَعَلْنَ – البقرة (240)

وَ نُنْشِئَكُمْ فِيْ مَا لَا تَعْلَمُوْنَ – الواقعة (61)

فِيْ مَا رَزَقْنٰكُمْ – الروم (28)

اِنَّ اللّٰهَ يَحْكُمُ بَيْنَهُمْ فِيْ مَا هُمْ فِيْهِ يَخْتَلِفُوْنَ – الزمر (3)

فِيْ مَا كَانُوْا فِيْهِ يَخْتَلِفُوْنَ – الزمر (46)

اَتُتْرَكُوْنَ فِيْ مَا هٰهُنَآ اٰمِنِيْنَ – الشعراء (146)

أَيْنَ مَا (أَيْنَمَا)

There are only two verses in the *Qur'an* in which these two words are written joint.

[89] فَأَيْنَمَا كَالنَّحْلِ صِلْ ....

(اي صِلْ فَأَيْنَمَا في البقرة كما صِلْتَه في سورة النحل)

فَاَيْنَمَا تُوَلُّوْا فَثَمَّ وَجْهُ اللّٰهِ – البقرة (115)

اَيْنَمَا يُوَجِّهْهُّ لَايَاْتِ بِخَيْرٍ – النحل (76)

But the *Masahif* differ in three verses.

[89] .... وَ [رَسْمُ اَيْنَمَا] مُخْتَلِفْ ... فِي الشُّعَرَا الأَحْزَابِ وَالنِّسَا وُصِفْ

وَ قِيْلَ لَهُمْ اَيْنَمَا كُنْتُمْ تَعْبُدُوْنَ – الشعراء (92)

أَيْنَمَا ثُقِفُوٓا أُخِذُوٓا – الاحزاب (61)

أَيْنَ مَا تَكُونُوٓا يُدْرِككُّمُ الْمَوْتُ – النساء (78)

In all other places they are written separately, according to all of the copies of the *Masahif*.

فَإِنْ لَمْ (فَإِلَّمْ)

The *Nun* is merged into the *Laam*, both in pronunciation and in writing, in verse 14 of *Surah Hud*. In all other places they are written separately.

[90] وَصِلْ فَإِلَّمْ [في سورة] هُودَ ....

فَإِلَّمْ يَسْتَجِيبُوٓا لَكُمْ – هود (14)

أَنْ لَنْ (أَلَّنْ)

The *Nun* is merged into the *Laam*, both in pronunciation and writing, in two verses of the *Qur'an*.

[90] .... [وَ صِلْ] أَلَّنْ نَجْعَلاَ ... [وَ أَلَّنْ] نَجْمَعَ ....

بَلْ زَعَمْتُمْ أَلَّنْ نَّجْعَلَ لَكُمْ مَّوْعِدًا – الكهف (48)

أَيَحْسَبُ الْإِنْسَانُ أَلَّنْ نَّجْمَعَ عِظَامَهُ - القيامة (3)

كَيْ لَا (كَيْلَا)

The *Yaa* is merged into the *Laam*, both in pronunciation and writing, in the following 4 verses:

[90] .... [وَ صِلْ] كَيْلاَ تَحْزَنُوا [وَ كَيْلاَ] تَأْسَوْا عَلَى

[91] .[وَ كَيْلاَ في سورة] حَجّ [وَ كَيْلاَ الذي بعده] عَلَيْكَ حَرَجٌ....... ... .

فَاَثَابَكُمْ غَمًّا بِغَمٍّ لِّكَيْلَا تَحْزَنُوْا – آل عمران (153)

لِّكَيْلَا تَأْسَوْا عَلٰى مَا فَاتَكُمْ – الحديد (23)

لِكَيْلَا يَعْلَمَ مِنْ بَعْدِ عِلْمٍ شَيْئًا – الحج (5)

وَ مَا مَلَكَتْ اَيْمَانُهُمْ لِكَيْلَا يَكُوْنَ عَلَيْكَ حَرَجٌ – الاحزاب (50)

عَنْ مَنْ	The *Nun* is written separately from the *Mim* in 2 verses, according to all *Masahif.*

[91] .. وَ[ثَبَتَ] قَطْعُهُمْ (اي ارباب الرسوم) ...[في موضعين و هما] عَنْ مَنْ يَشَاءُ [وَ] مَنْ تَوَلّٰى

وَ يَصْرِفُهٗ عَنْ مَّنْ يَّشَآءُ – النور (43)

فَاَعْرِضْ عَنْ مَّنْ تَوَلّٰى – النجم (29)

يَوْمَ هُمْ	The *Mim* is written separately from the *Haa* in 2 verses, according to all *Masahif.*

[91] ....[وَ اقْطَعْ] يَوْمَ هُمْ

يَوْمَ هُمْ بٰرِزُوْنَ – غافر (16)

يَوْمَ هُمْ عَلَى النَّارِ يُفْتَنُوْنَ – (13)

لامُ الجر عن المجرور	The *Laam Jaarrah* is written separately from the *Majroor* noun after it in 4 verses, according to all *Masahif.* In all other verses they are joint.

[92] و [اِقْطَعْ] مَالِ هٰذَا [في موضعين] وَ [مَالِ] الَّذِينَ [وَ مَالِ] هٰؤُلَاءِ ... .

(اي اِقْطَعْ لَامِ الْجَرِّ عن مجرورِهَا في اربعةِ مواضعَ)

مَالِ هٰذَا الْكِتٰبِ – الكهف (49)

وَ قَالُوْا مَالِ هٰذَا الرَّسُوْلِ – الفرقان (7)

فَمَالِ الَّذِيْنَ كَفَرُوْا – المعارج (36)

فَمَالِ هٰٓؤُلَآءِ الْقَوْمِ لَا يَكَادُوْنَ يَفْقَهُوْنَ حَدِيْثًا – النساء (78)

لَاتَ حِيْنَ

The *Taa* is connected to the word حِيْنَ after it in the *Mushaf* that *Sayyiduna Uthman* used to recite from (لَاتَحِيْنَ). However, connecting it to حِيْنَ is weak and the correct way of writing it is to separate the two, just like it is written in all other *Masahif*.

[92] .... تَحِينَ في الإِمَامِ صِلْ وَوُهِلَا

(اي صِلْ تائَه بحَاءِ حِيْنَ كما في مصحف الامام و وُهِّلَ هذا القولُ اي ضُعِّفَ وَ الاَصَحُّ هو القَطعُ لانه مفصولة في المصاحف السبعة)

وَّ لَاتَ حِيْنَ مَنَاصٍ – ص (3)

كَالُوهُمْ (كَالُوْا & هُمْ)

وَزَنُوهُمْ (وَزَنُوا & هُمْ)

The words كَالُوْا and وَزَنُوا both, originally, had an *Alif* after the *Waw*. However, since they are written connected to the pronoun هُمْ after them, the *Alif* has been dropped.

[93] وَ وَزَنُوهُمْ [وَ] كَالُوهُمْ صِلِ ... .

وَ اِذَا كَالُوْهُمْ اَوْ وَّزَنُوْهُمْ يُخْسِرُوْنَ – المطففين (3)

If they were written separately, then the *Alif* would have remained as it has in the following verse:

وَ إِذَا مَا غَضِبُوا هُمْ يَغْفِرُونَ – سورة الشورى

ال & الاسم

Likewise, the *Laam* of *Ta'rif* should not be separated from the noun after it.

[93] .... كذا [لَا تَفْصِلْ مدخولَ لامِ التَّعريف] من أل ......

الْحَمْدُ لِلّٰهِ – الفاتحة (1)

يا & منادى

Likewise, the *Yaa* used for calling should not be separated from the noun after it. For example:

[93] .... و [لَا تفْصِلْ مدخولَ يَا النِدَاءِ عن] يا ....

يٰٓاَيُّهَا النَّاسُ اعْبُدُوْا رَبَّكُمُ – البقرة (21)

وَ قُلْنَا يٰاٰدَمُ اسْكُنْ اَنْتَ وَ زَوْجُكَ الْجَنَّةَ – البقرة (35)

قَالَ يٰبُنَيَّ لَا تَقْصُصْ رُءْيَاكَ – يوسف (5)

هَاءُ التَّنْبِيْهِ & الاسم

Likewise, the *Haa* used to draw attention should not be separated from the noun it is on.

[93] .... وَ هَا [التنبيهِ] لا تَفْصِلِ [هَا عن مدخولها]

هٰٓؤُلَآءِ اِنْ كُنْتُمْ صٰدِقِيْنَ – البقرة (31)

بِاَمْرِهِمْ هٰذَا – يوسف (15)

Recitation Practice

Recite the following Surah and identify all of the rules of *Nun Sakinah* and *Tanween*, *Mim Sakinah*, *Mudud*, *Tafkhim* and *Tarqiq*.

بِسۡمِ اللّٰهِ الرَّحۡمٰنِ الرَّحِيۡمِ ﴿﴾

إِذَا الشَّمۡسُ كُوِّرَتۡ ﴿١﴾ وَإِذَا النُّجُوۡمُ انۡكَدَرَتۡ ﴿٢﴾ وَإِذَا الۡجِبَالُ سُيِّرَتۡ ﴿٣﴾
وَ إِذَا الۡعِشَارُ عُطِّلَتۡ ﴿٤﴾ وَ إِذَا الۡوُحُوۡشُ حُشِرَتۡ ﴿٥﴾ وَ إِذَا الۡبِحَارُ
سُجِّرَتۡ ﴿٦﴾ وَ إِذَا النُّفُوۡسُ زُوِّجَتۡ ﴿٧﴾ وَ إِذَا الۡمَوۡءٗدَةُ سُئِلَتۡ ﴿٨﴾ بِاَيِّ ذَنۡۢبٍ
قُتِلَتۡ ﴿٩﴾ وَإِذَا الصُّحُفُ نُشِرَتۡ ﴿١٠﴾ وَإِذَا السَّمَآءُ كُشِطَتۡ ﴿١١﴾ وَإِذَا الۡجَحِيۡمُ
سُعِّرَتۡ ﴿١٢﴾ وَ إِذَا الۡجَنَّةُ اُزۡلِفَتۡ ﴿١٣﴾ عَلِمَتۡ نَفۡسٌ مَّآ اَحۡضَرَتۡ ﴿١٤﴾ فَلَآ اُقۡسِمُ
بِالۡخُنَّسِ ﴿١٥﴾ الۡجَوَارِ الۡكُنَّسِ ﴿١٦﴾ وَ الَّيۡلِ إِذَا عَسۡعَسَ ﴿١٧﴾ وَ الصُّبۡحِ إِذَا تَنَفَّسَ
﴿١٨﴾ إِنَّهٗ لَقَوۡلُ رَسُوۡلٍ كَرِيۡمٍ ﴿١٩﴾ ذِیۡ قُوَّةٍ عِنۡدَ ذِی الۡعَرۡشِ مَكِيۡنٍ ﴿٢٠﴾ مُّطَاعٍ ثَمَّ
اَمِيۡنٍ ﴿٢١﴾ وَ مَا صَاحِبُكُمۡ بِمَجۡنُوۡنٍ ﴿٢٢﴾ وَ لَقَدۡ رَاٰهُ بِالۡاُفُقِ الۡمُبِيۡنِ ﴿٢٣﴾ وَ مَا هُوَ
عَلَى الۡغَيۡبِ بِضَنِيۡنٍ ﴿٢٤﴾ وَ مَا هُوَ بِقَوۡلِ شَيۡطٰنٍ رَّجِيۡمٍ ﴿٢٥﴾ فَاَيۡنَ تَذۡهَبُوۡنَ ﴿٢٦﴾
اِنۡ هُوَ اِلَّا ذِكۡرٌ لِّلۡعٰلَمِيۡنَ ﴿٢٧﴾ لِمَنۡ شَآءَ مِنۡكُمۡ اَنۡ يَّسۡتَقِيۡمَ ﴿٢٨﴾ وَ مَا تَشَآءُوۡنَ
اِلَّآ اَنۡ يَّشَآءَ اللّٰهُ رَبُّ الۡعٰلَمِيۡنَ ﴿٢٩﴾

باب التاءات

Taa

[94] وَ رَحْمَتُ الزُّخْرُفِ بِالتَا زَبَرَهْ ... اَلاعْرَافِ رُومٍ هُودَ كَافَ الْبَقَرَهْ

[95] نِعْمَتُهَا ثَلاثُ نَحْلٍ إِبْرَهَمْ ... مَعًا أَخِيْرَاتٌ عُقُودُ الثَّانِ هَمْ

[96] لُقْمَانَ ثُمَّ فَاطِرٌ كَالطُّور ... عِمْرَانَ لَعْنَتَ بِهَا وَالنُّور

[97] وَ امْرَأَتُ يُوسُفَ عِمْرَانَ الْقَصَصْ ... تَحْرِيْمَ مَعْصِيَتْ بِقَدْ سَمِعْ يُخَصْ

[98] شَجَرَتَ الدُّخَانِ سُنَّتْ فَاطِر ... كُلًّا وَّالَانْفَالِ وَأُخْرٰى غَافِر

[99] قُرَّتُ عَيْنٍ جَنَّتٌ فِي وَقَعَتْ ... فِطْرَتْ بَقِيَّتْ وَابْنَتٌ وَّكَلِمَتْ

[100] أَوْسَطَ الَاعْرَافِ وَكُلُّ مَااخْتُلِفْ ... جَمْعًا وَّفَرْدًا فِيْهِ بِالتَّاءِ عُرِفْ

THE TA OF FEMININE

The *Ta* of feminine is written in two different ways in the *Qur'an*:

1. Aa a long *Ta* (ت), known as التاء المجرورة
2. As a round *Ta* (ة), known as التاء المربوطة

WAQF

When doing *Waqf*, the round *Ta* is recited as a *Sakin Ha*. However, the Imams of *Tajweed* differ on the manner of *Waqf* on the long *Ta*. *Imam Ibn Kathir, Abu 'Amr* and *Kassa'i* pronounce it like a *Sakin Ha* when doing *Waqf*. But the remaining Imams recite it like a *Sakin Ta*. Therefore, it is important for the reciter to know the places of long *Ta* in the *Qur'an*, so that they are able to pronounce it properly according to the *Riwayah* they are reciting it in.

In the above passage, *Imam ibn al-Jazari* ﷺ highlights the places in *Qur'an* that contain the long *Ta*. They are as follows:

Word	Verses
رَحْمَتُ	[94] وَ رَحْمَتُ الزُّخْرُفِ بِالتَا زَبَرَهْ (اي كَتَبَه سيدنا عثمان) ... [وَفي] الأَعْرَافِ [وَ] رُومٍ [وَ] هُودَ [وَ] كَافَ [وَ] الْبَقَرَهْ اَهُمْ يَقْسِمُوْنَ رَحْمَتَ رَبِّكَ – الزخرف (32) وَ رَحْمَتُ رَبِّكَ خَيْرٌ مِّمَّا يَجْمَعُوْنَ – الزخرف (32) اِنَّ رَحْمَتَ اللهِ قَرِيْبٌ مِّنَ الْمُحْسِنِيْنَ – الاعراف (56) فَانْظُرْ اِلَى اٰثٰرِ رَحْمَتِ اللهِ – الروم (50) رَحْمَتُ اللهِ وَ بَرَكٰتُهٗ عَلَيْكُمْ اَهْلَ الْبَيْتِ – هود (73) ذِكْرُ رَحْمَتِ رَبِّكَ عَبْدَهٗ زَكَرِيَّا – مريم (2)

أُولَٰٓئِكَ يَرۡجُوۡنَ رَحۡمَتَ اللّٰهِ – البقرة (218)	
[95] نِعۡمَتُهَا (اي البقرة) [وَ] ثَلاثُ نَحۡلٍ [وَ] إِبۡرٰهَمْ ... مَعًا أَخِيرَاتٌ (اي و هُنَّ أَخِيرَاتٌ من السورتين اِحترازًا من أوائل النحل ز أول إبراهيم) [وَ] عُقُودُ (اي المائدة) [في الموضع] الثَّانِ [فيها المقرون بِـ] هَمْ [96] . [وَنِعْمَتُ] لُقۡمَانُ ثُمَّ فَاطِرٌ كَالطُّورِ ... [وَ] عِمۡرَانَ .... وَّ اذۡكُرُوۡا نِعۡمَتَ اللّٰهِ عَلَيۡكُمۡ – البقرة (231) وَ بِنِعۡمَتِ اللّٰهِ هُمۡ يَكۡفُرُوۡنَ – النحل (72) يَعۡرِفُوۡنَ نِعۡمَتَ اللّٰهِ ثُمَّ يُنۡكِرُوۡنَهَا – النحل (83) وَّ اشۡكُرُوۡا نِعۡمَتَ اللّٰهِ – النحل (114) الَّذِيۡنَ بَدَّلُوۡا نِعۡمَتَ اللّٰهِ كُفۡرًا – ابراهيم (28) وَ اِنۡ تَعُدُّوۡا نِعۡمَتَ اللّٰهِ لَا تُحۡصُوۡهَا – ابراهيم (34) يٰۤاَيُّهَا الَّذِيۡنَ اٰمَنُوا اذۡكُرُوۡا نِعۡمَتَ اللّٰهِ عَلَيۡكُمۡ اِذۡ هَمَّ قَوۡمٌ – المائدة –العقود (11) اَلَمۡ تَرَ اَنَّ الۡفُلۡكَ تَجۡرِىۡ فِى الۡبَحۡرِ بِنِعۡمَتِ اللّٰهِ – لقمان (31) يٰۤاَيُّهَا النَّاسُ اذۡكُرُوۡا نِعۡمَتَ اللّٰهِ عَلَيۡكُمۡ – فاطر (3) فَذَكِّرۡ فَمَاۤ اَنۡتَ بِنِعۡمَتِ رَبِّكَ بِكَاهِنٍ وَّ لَا مَجۡنُوۡنٍ – الطور (29) وَ اذۡكُرُوۡا نِعۡمَتَ اللّٰهِ عَلَيۡكُمۡ – آل عمران (103)	نِعۡمَتُ
[96] .... [وَ أَنَّ لَفۡظَ] لَعۡنَتَ [مَرسومٌ بالتاء المجرورة] بِهَا (اي بِآل عمران) وَالنُّورِ فَنَجۡعَلۡ لَّعۡنَتَ اللّٰهِ عَلَى الۡكٰذِبِيۡنَ – آل عمران (61)	لَعۡنَتَ

	وَ الْخَامِسَةُ اَنَّ لَعۡنَتَ اللّٰهِ عَلَيۡهِ – النور (7)
امْرَأَتُ	[97] وَ [أَنَّ لَفْظَ] امْرَأَت [مجرورة في الموضعين في سورة] يُوسُفَ [وَ] عِمْرَانَ [وَ] الْقَصَصْ ... [وَثلاثةِ مَوَاضِعَ في] تَحْرِيْمَ .... وَ قَالَ نِسۡوَةٌ فِي الۡمَدِيۡنَةِ امۡرَاَتُ الۡعَزِيۡزِ تُرَاوِدُ فَتٰٮهَا عَنۡ نَّفۡسِهٖ - يوسف (30) قَالَتِ امۡرَاَتُ الۡعَزِيۡزِ الۡـٰٔنَ حَصۡحَصَ الۡحَقُّ – يوسف (51) اِذۡ قَالَتِ امۡرَاَتُ عِمۡرٰنَ رَبِّ اِنِّىۡ نَذَرۡتُ لَكَ مَا فِىۡ بَطۡنِىۡ مُحَرَّرًا – آل عمران (35) وَ قَالَتِ امۡرَاَتُ فِرۡعَوۡنَ قُرَّتُ عَيۡنٍ لِّىۡ وَ لَكَ – القصص (9) ضَرَبَ اللّٰهُ مَثَلًا لِّلَّذِيۡنَ كَفَرُوا امۡرَاَتَ نُوۡحٍ وَّ امۡرَاَتَ لُوۡطٍ - التحريم (10) وَ ضَرَبَ اللّٰهُ مَثَلًا لِّلَّذِيۡنَ اٰمَنُوا امۡرَاَتَ فِرۡعَوۡنَ – التحريم (11)
مَعۡصِيَت	[97] .... مَعْصِيَتْ بِ [مَوْضِعَي] قَدْ سَمِعْ (اي المجادلة) يُخَصْ (اي أَنَّ لَفْظَ مَعۡصِيَت بالتاء المجرورة مَخْصُوْصٌ بِمَوْضِعَيْ الْمُجَادَلَةِ) وَ يَتَنٰجَوۡنَ بِالۡاِثۡمِ وَ الۡعُدۡوَانِ وَ مَعۡصِيَتِ الرَّسُوۡلِ – المجادلة (8) فَلَا تَتَنَاجَوۡا بِالۡاِثۡمِ وَ الۡعُدۡوَانِ وَ مَعۡصِيَتِ الرَّسُوۡلِ – المجادلة (9)
شَجَرَت	[98] . [يُخَصُّ لَفْظُ] شَجَرَت [بالتاء المجرورة بموضع واحد في] الدُّخَانِ...... ... . اِنَّ شَجَرَتَ الزَّقُّوۡمِ – الدخان (43)

سُنَّتَ	[98] .... [وَكَذٰلِكَ] سُنَّتَ فَاطِرِ ... كُلًّا (و هو ثلاثة مواضع) وَ الْأَنْفَالِ وَأُخْرٰى غَافِرِ فَهَلْ يَنْظُرُوْنَ اِلَّا سُنَّتَ الْاَوَّلِيْنَ فَلَنْ تَجِدَ لِسُنَّتِ اللّٰهِ تَبْدِيْلًا وَ لَنْ تَجِدَ لِسُنَّتِ اللّٰهِ تَحْوِيْلًا – فاطر (43) فَقَدْ مَضَتْ سُنَّتُ الْاَوَّلِيْنَ – الانفال (38) سُنَّتَ اللّٰهِ الَّتِيْ قَدْ خَلَتْ فِيْ عِبَادِهٖ - غافر (85)
قُرَّتُ	[99] .[وَكَذٰلِكَ] قُرَّتُ عَيْنٍ [في سورة القصص تكتب بالتاء المجرورة]....... ... . وَ قَالَتِ امْرَاَتُ فِرْعَوْنَ قُرَّتُ عَيْنٍ لِّيْ وَ لَكَ – القصص (9)
جَنَّتُ	[99] ....[وَ] جَنَّتُ فِي وَقَعَتْ (اي في سورة الواقعة) .... فَرَوْحٌ وَّ رَيْحَانٌ وَّ جَنَّتُ نَعِيْمٍ – الواقعة (89)
فِطْرَتَ	[99] ....[وَ] فِطْرَتَ [في الروم]............... فِطْرَتَ اللّٰهِ الَّتِيْ فَطَرَ النَّاسَ عَلَيْهَا – الروم (30)
بَقِيَّتُ	[99] .... [وَ] بَقِيَّتُ [في هود]........... بَقِيَّتُ اللّٰهِ خَيْرٌ لَّكُمْ اِنْ كُنْتُمْ مُّؤْمِنِيْنَ – هود (86)
وَابْنَتُ	[99] ....[وَ] وَابْنَتُ [في التحريم]......... وَ مَرْيَمَ ابْنَتَ عِمْرٰنَ الَّتِيْ اَحْصَنَتْ فَرْجَهَا – التحريم (12)
كَلِمَتُ	[99] .... وَ كَلِمَتُ [100] أَوْسَطَ الْاَعْرَافِ....... ... . وَ تَمَّتْ كَلِمَتُ رَبِّكَ الْحُسْنٰى- الاعراف (137)

[100] .... وَكُلُّ مَا اخْتُلِفْ ... جَمْعًا وَفَرْدًا فِيْهِ بِالتَّاءِ عُرِفْ

And all the places, where the Masahif have a difference concerning a word being plural or singular, they are known to be with a Ta Majroorah.

In other words, if there is a difference between the *Imams* of *Qira'ah* concerning whether a particular word ending with a *Ta* is singular or plural, and some recite it in the plural form, whilst others recite it in the singular form. Then that *Ta* is written as a long *Ta*. For example:

وَأَلْقُوهُ فِى غَيَٰبَتِ الْجُبِّ – يوسف (10)

Recitation Practice

Recite the following Surah and identify all of the rules of *Nun Sakinah* and *Tanween*, *Mim Sakinah*, *Mudud*, *Tafkhim* and *Tarqiq*.

بِسْمِ اللّٰهِ الرَّحْمٰنِ الرَّحِيْمِ ۝

وَسِيْقَ الَّذِيْنَ كَفَرُوْٓا اِلٰى جَهَنَّمَ زُمَرًا ۭ حَتّٰٓى اِذَا جَاۗءُوْهَا فُتِحَتْ اَبْوَابُهَا وَ
قَالَ لَهُمْ خَزَنَتُهَآ اَلَمْ يَاْتِكُمْ رُسُلٌ مِّنْكُمْ يَتْلُوْنَ عَلَيْكُمْ اٰيٰتِ رَبِّكُمْ وَ
يُنْذِرُوْنَكُمْ لِقَاۗءَ يَوْمِكُمْ هٰذَا ۭ قَالُوْا بَلٰى وَلٰكِنْ حَقَّتْ كَلِمَةُ الْعَذَابِ عَلَى
الْكٰفِرِيْنَ ۝٧١ قِيْلَ ادْخُلُوْٓا اَبْوَابَ جَهَنَّمَ خٰلِدِيْنَ فِيْهَا ۚ فَبِئْسَ مَثْوَى
الْمُتَكَبِّرِيْنَ ۝٧٢ وَسِيْقَ الَّذِيْنَ اتَّقَوْا رَبَّهُمْ اِلَى الْجَنَّةِ زُمَرًا ۭ حَتّٰٓى اِذَا
جَاۗءُوْهَا وَ فُتِحَتْ اَبْوَابُهَا وَ قَالَ لَهُمْ خَزَنَتُهَا سَلٰمٌ عَلَيْكُمْ طِبْتُمْ
فَادْخُلُوْهَا خٰلِدِيْنَ ۝٧٣ وَ قَالُوا الْحَمْدُ لِلّٰهِ الَّذِيْ صَدَقَنَا وَعْدَهٗ وَ اَوْرَثَنَا
الْاَرْضَ نَتَبَوَّاُ مِنَ الْجَنَّةِ حَيْثُ نَشَاۗءُ ۚ فَنِعْمَ اَجْرُ الْعٰمِلِيْنَ ۝٧٤

باب همز الوصل

Hamzat ul-Wasl

[101] وَابْدَأْ بِهَمْزِ الْوَصْلِ مِنْ فِعْلٍ بِضَمْ ... إِنْ كَانَ ثَالِثٌ مِّنَ الْفِعْلِ يُضَمْ

[102] وَاكْسِرْهُ حَالَ الْكَسْرِ وَالْفَتْحِ وَفِي ... الاَسْمَاءِ غَيْرِ اللاَّمِ كَسْرُهَا وَفِي

[103] اِبْنٍ مَّعَ ابْنَةِ امْرِئٍ وَّ اثْنَيْن ... وَ امْرَأَةٍ وَّ اسْمٍ مَّعَ اثْنَتَيْن

HAMZAT UL-WASL

This is a *Hamzah* that is pronounced when it comes at the start of speech, but not when it appears in the middle. For example:

نِّصْفَهٗٓ اَوِ انْقُصْ مِنْهُ قَلِيْلًا – المزمل (3)

The word أنْقُصْ has a *Hamzat ul-Wasl* at the start. However, since it is in the middle of the verse and not at the start, it is silent. Instead, the *Waw* preceding it is connected to the *Nun* after the *Hamzah*.

HAMZAT UL-WASL IN VERBS

It only comes before the following types of verbs:

1. Verbs that have 5 letters in the past tense: اِنْطَلَقَ
2. Verbs that have 6 letters in the past tense: اِسْتَخْرَجَ
3. The Imperative tense: أُنْظُرْ

In the past tense it is always *Maksoor*, unless the verb is in the Passive voice (مَجْهُول), in which case it will be *Madhmoom*. As for the Imperative tense, the author asks the reader to look at the third letter to determine the vowel of the *Hamzah*. If it has a *Dhammah*, then the *Hamzah* will also have a *Dhammah*. But if it has a *Kasrah* or a *Fathah*, then the *Hamzah* will have a *Kasrah*. For example:

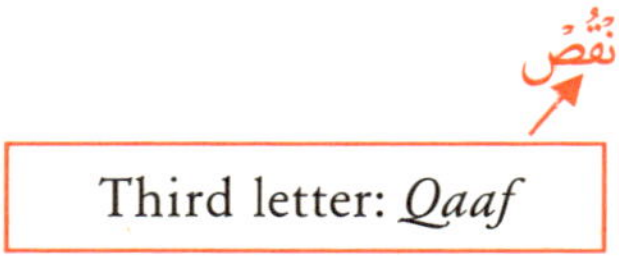

In this example, since the *Qaaf* has a *Dhammah*, the *Hamzah* will also be recited with a *Dhammah*.

Imam ibn al-Jazari ﷺ says:

[101] وَابْدَأْ بِهَمْزِ الْوَصْلِ مِنْ فِعْلٍ بِضَمْ ... إِنْ كَانَ ثَالِثٌ مِنَ الفِعْلِ يُضَمْ

Begin the Hamzat ul-Wasl in a verb with a Dhammah
If the third [letter] in the verb has a Dhammah

[102] وَاكْسِرْهُ حَالَ الْكَسْرِ وَالْفَتْحِ ... .

And give it a Kasrah, when [it is in the state of] Maksoor or a Maftooh.

HAMZAT UL-WASL IN NOUNS

Hamzat ul-Wasl in nouns is always *Maksoor*, except when they have the *Laam* of *Ta'rif* (ال) connected to them, in which case the *Hamzat ul-Wasl* is not pronounced as it is no longer at the start.

The author says:

[102] .... وَفِي ... الأَسْمَاءِ غَيْرِ اللاَّمِ كَسْرُهَا وَفِيٌّ

And in the nouns, other than [those that have] ال*, a Kasrah is plenty*

Note: the word وَفِيٌّ is *Ism Fa'il* on the scale of فَعِيلٌ , i.e. وَافٍ (plenty).

The author ﷺ then provides examples of nouns that have a *Hamzat ul-Wasl* at the start. He says:

[103] ابْنٍ مَعَ ابْنَةِ امْرِئٍ وَ اثْنَيْنِ ... وَ امْرَأَةٍ وَ اسْمٍ مَعَ اثْنَتَيْنِ

Such as ابْنٍ *with* ابْنَةِ *,* امرئ *and* اثنين
And امْرَأَةٍ *,* اسْمٍ *with* اثْنَتَيْنِ

Note: The *Hamzat ul-Wasl* preceding the *Laam* of *Ta'rif* is always *Maftooh*.

Recitation Practice

Recite the following Surah and identify all of the rules of *Nun Sakinah* and *Tanween*, *Mim Sakinah*, *Mudud*, *Tafkhim* and *Tarqiq*.

بِسْمِ اللّٰهِ الرَّحْمٰنِ الرَّحِيْمِ ﴿﴾

الرَّحْمٰنُ ۙ﴿١﴾ عَلَّمَ الْقُرْاٰنَ ؕ﴿٢﴾ خَلَقَ الْاِنْسَانَ ۙ﴿٣﴾ عَلَّمَهُ الْبَيَانَ ﴿٤﴾ اَلشَّمْسُ وَ
الْقَمَرُ بِحُسْبَانٍ ۪﴿٥﴾ وَّ النَّجْمُ وَ الشَّجَرُ يَسْجُدٰنِ ﴿٦﴾ وَ السَّمَآءَ رَفَعَهَا وَ وَضَعَ
الْمِيْزَانَ ۙ﴿٧﴾ اَلَّا تَطْغَوْا فِي الْمِيْزَانِ ﴿٨﴾ وَ اَقِيْمُوا الْوَزْنَ بِالْقِسْطِ وَ لَا
تُخْسِرُوا الْمِيْزَانَ ﴿٩﴾ وَ الْاَرْضَ وَضَعَهَا لِلْاَنَامِ ۙ﴿١٠﴾ فِيْهَا فَاكِهَةٌ ۪ۙ وَّ النَّخْلُ
ذَاتُ الْاَكْمَامِ ۖ﴿١١﴾ وَ الْحَبُّ ذُو الْعَصْفِ وَ الرَّيْحَانُ ۚ﴿١٢﴾ فَبِاَيِّ اٰلَآءِ رَبِّكُمَا
تُكَذِّبٰنِ ﴿١٣﴾ خَلَقَ الْاِنْسَانَ مِنْ صَلْصَالٍ كَالْفَخَّارِ ۙ﴿١٤﴾ وَ خَلَقَ الْجَآنَّ مِنْ
مَّارِجٍ مِّنْ نَّارٍ ۚ﴿١٥﴾ فَبِاَيِّ اٰلَآءِ رَبِّكُمَا تُكَذِّبٰنِ ﴿١٦﴾ رَبُّ الْمَشْرِقَيْنِ وَ رَبُّ
الْمَغْرِبَيْنِ ۚ﴿١٧﴾ فَبِاَيِّ اٰلَآءِ رَبِّكُمَا تُكَذِّبٰنِ ﴿١٨﴾ مَرَجَ الْبَحْرَيْنِ يَلْتَقِيٰنِ ۙ﴿١٩﴾
بَيْنَهُمَا بَرْزَخٌ لَّا يَبْغِيٰنِ ۚ﴿٢٠﴾ فَبِاَيِّ اٰلَآءِ رَبِّكُمَا تُكَذِّبٰنِ ﴿٢١﴾ يَخْرُجُ مِنْهُمَا
اللُّؤْلُؤُ وَ الْمَرْجَانُ ۚ﴿٢٢﴾ فَبِاَيِّ اٰلَآءِ رَبِّكُمَا تُكَذِّبٰنِ ﴿٢٣﴾ وَ لَهُ الْجَوَارِ
الْمُنْشَئٰتُ فِي الْبَحْرِ كَالْاَعْلَامِ ۚ﴿٢٤﴾ فَبِاَيِّ اٰلَآءِ رَبِّكُمَا تُكَذِّبٰنِ ﴿٢٥﴾ كُلُّ مَنْ
عَلَيْهَا فَانٍ ۖۚ﴿٢٦﴾ وَّ يَبْقٰى وَجْهُ رَبِّكَ ذُو الْجَلٰلِ وَ الْاِكْرَامِ ۚ﴿٢٧﴾

باب الوقف على أواخر الكلم

Waqf

[104] وَحَاذِرِ الْوَقْفَ بِكُلِّ الْحَرَكَهْ ... إلاَّ إِذَا رُمْتَ فَبَعْضُ الْحَرَكَهْ

[105] إِلَّا بِفَتْحٍ أَوْ بِنَصْبٍ وَّأَشِمْ ... إِشَارَةً بِالضَّمِّ فِي رَفْعٍ وَّضَمْ

IMPORTANT TERMINOLOGY

Rawm: الرَّوْمُ هُوَ عِبَارَةٌ عَنْ النُّطْقِ بِبَعْضِ الْحَرَكَةِ و قَالَ بَعْضُهُمْ هُوَ تَضْعِيْفُ الصَّوْتِ بِالْحَرَكَةِ حَتَّى يَذْهَبَ مُعْظَمُهَا و يَسْمَعُهَا الْقَرِيْبُ دُونَ الْبَعِيْدِ (ابن يالوشه)

Rawm consists of pronouncing the vowel partially. Others have described it as making the sound of the vowel weak, so that most of the sound is missing. In effect, only the people sitting near can hear the sound of the vowel and not someone sitting at a distance.

Ishmaam: الاشمام هُوَ أَنْ تَضُمَّ شَفَتَيْكَ بَعْدَ الْإِسْكَانِ كَهَيْئَتِهِمَا عِنْدَ التَّقْبِيْلِ إِشَارَةً الى الضَّمِّ و تَتْرُكَ بَيْنَهُمَا بَعْضَ انْفِرَاجٍ لِيَخْرُجَ النَّفَس فَيَرَاهُمَا الْمُخَاطَبُ مَضْمُومَتَيْنِ فَيَعْلَمُ أَنَّكَ أَردتَّ بِضَمِّهِمَا الاِشَارَةَ الى حَرَكَةِ آخِرِ الْكَلِمَةِ الْمَوْقُوْفِ عَلَيْهَا فَهُوَ شَيءٌ يُدْرَكُ بِالعَيْنِ دُونَ الْأُذُنِ (ملا على القارئ – ابن يالوشه)

Ishmaam is to join the lips after making the letter *Sakin*, in a manner that is used to kiss, in order to indicate to the *Dhammah* and a small gap is left in the lips to allow the air to pass. When the person listening to the recitation sees the lips, they know that the word has a *Dhammah* at the end. *Ishmaam* is something that is seen and not heard.

The author ﵀ says:

[104] وَحَاذِرِ الْوَقْفَ بِكُلِّ الحَرَكَهْ ... إِلاَّ إِذَا رُمْتَ فَبَعْضُ حَرَكَهْ

And be careful of stopping with a complete vowel
Except when you perform Rawm, then partial vowel [is permissible]

[105] إِلاَّ بِفَتْحٍ أَوْ بِنَصْبٍ وَأَشِمْ ... إِشَارَةً بِالضَّمِّ فِي رَفْعٍ وَضَمْ

Unless [the word ends] with a Fathah or Nasb. And perform Ishmaam
By indicating to a Dhammah, [when stopping] on a Raf' or Dhammah

See the page for the explanation in the form of a diagram.

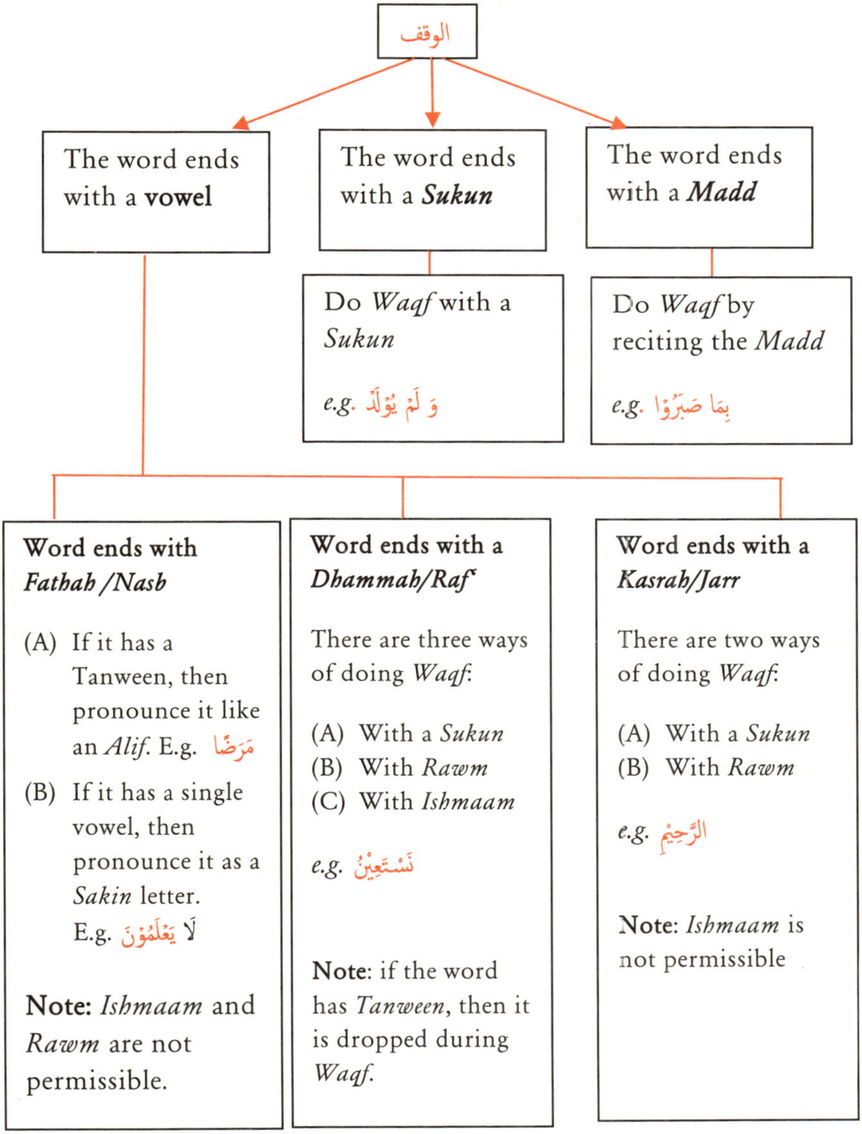
الوقف
The word ends with a **vowel**
The word ends with a ***Sukun***
The word ends with a ***Madd***
Do *Waqf* with a *Sukun*
e.g. وَ لَمْ يُوْلَدْ
Do *Waqf* by reciting the *Madd*
e.g. بِمَا صَبَرُوْا
Word ends with *Fathah /Nasb*
(A) If it has a Tanween, then pronounce it like an *Alif*. E.g. مَرَضًا
(B) If it has a single vowel, then pronounce it as a *Sakin* letter. E.g. لاَ يَعْلَمُوْنَ
Note: *Ishmaam* and *Rawm* are not permissible.
Word ends with a *Dhammah/Raf'*
There are three ways of doing *Waqf*:
(A) With a *Sukun*
(B) With *Rawm*
(C) With *Ishmaam*
e.g. نَسْتَعِيْنُ
Note: if the word has *Tanween*, then it is dropped during *Waqf*.
Word ends with a *Kasrah/Jarr*
There are two ways of doing *Waqf*:
(A) With a *Sukun*
(B) With *Rawm*
e.g. الرَّحِيْمِ
Note: *Ishmaam* is not permissible

Recitation Practice

Recite the following Surah and identify all of the rules of *Nun Sakinah* and *Tanween*, *Mim Sakinah*, *Mudud*, *Tafkhim* and *Tarqiq*.

بِسْمِ اللّٰهِ الرَّحْمٰنِ الرَّحِيْمِ ﴿﴾

يٰۤاَيُّهَا الَّذِيْنَ اٰمَنُوا اتَّقُوا اللّٰهَ وَ لْتَنْظُرْ نَفْسٌ مَّا قَدَّمَتْ لِغَدٍۚ وَ اتَّقُوا اللّٰهَؕ اِنَّ
اللّٰهَ خَبِيْرٌۢ بِمَا تَعْمَلُوْنَ ﴿١٨﴾ وَ لَا تَكُوْنُوْا كَالَّذِيْنَ نَسُوا اللّٰهَ فَاَنْسٰىهُمْ
اَنْفُسَهُمْؕ اُولٰٓىِٕكَ هُمُ الْفٰسِقُوْنَ ﴿١٩﴾ لَا يَسْتَوِيْۤ اَصْحٰبُ النَّارِ وَ اَصْحٰبُ
الْجَنَّةِؕ اَصْحٰبُ الْجَنَّةِ هُمُ الْفَآىِٕزُوْنَ ﴿٢٠﴾ لَوْ اَنْزَلْنَا هٰذَا الْقُرْاٰنَ عَلٰى جَبَلٍ
لَّرَاَيْتَهٗ خٰشِعًا مُّتَصَدِّعًا مِّنْ خَشْيَةِ اللّٰهِؕ وَ تِلْكَ الْاَمْثٰلُ نَضْرِبُهَا لِلنَّاسِ
لَعَلَّهُمْ يَتَفَكَّرُوْنَ ﴿٢١﴾ هُوَ اللّٰهُ الَّذِيْ لَاۤ اِلٰهَ اِلَّا هُوَۚ عٰلِمُ الْغَيْبِ وَ الشَّهٰدَةِۚ
هُوَ الرَّحْمٰنُ الرَّحِيْمُ ﴿٢٢﴾ هُوَ اللّٰهُ الَّذِيْ لَاۤ اِلٰهَ اِلَّا هُوَۚ اَلْمَلِكُ الْقُدُّوْسُ
السَّلٰمُ الْمُؤْمِنُ الْمُهَيْمِنُ الْعَزِيْزُ الْجَبَّارُ الْمُتَكَبِّرُؕ سُبْحٰنَ اللّٰهِ عَمَّا
يُشْرِكُوْنَ ﴿٢٣﴾ هُوَ اللّٰهُ الْخٰلِقُ الْبَارِئُ الْمُصَوِّرُ لَهُ الْاَسْمَآءُ الْحُسْنٰىؕ يُسَبِّحُ
لَهٗ مَا فِي السَّمٰوٰتِ وَ الْاَرْضِۚ وَ هُوَ الْعَزِيْزُ الْحَكِيْمُ ﴿٢٤﴾

الخَاتِمَة

The Ending

[106] وَقَدْ تَقَضَّى نَظْمِيَ المُقَدِّمَهْ ... مِنِّي لِقَارِئِ الْقُرآنِ تَقْدِمَهْ

My poem 'al-Muqaddimah' has completed
[It is] a gift from me to the reciter of the Qur'an

[107] أَبْيَاتُهَا قَافٌ وَزَايٌ فِي الْعَدَدْ ... مَنْ يُحْسِنِ التَّجْوِيدَ يَظْفَرْ بِالرَّشَدْ

Its couplets are Qaaf and Zay in number (i.e. 107)
Whosoever perfects [their] Tajweed will be successful in guidance

[108] وَالْحَمْدُ للهِ لَهَا خِتَامُ ... ثُمَّ الصَّلَاةُ بَعْدُ وَالسَّلَامُ

And all praise is for Allah upon its completion
Then Salutations after, and Salaam be...

[109] عَلَى النَّبِيِّ الْمُصْطَفَى وَآلِهِ ... وَصَحْبِهِ وَتَابِعِي مِنْوَالِهِ

Upon the chosen prophet, his family,
His companions and those who follow his path

Many commentators on this poem, such as *Mulla Ali Qari* ﵀ , have missed out line 107. Likewise, others have said line 109 is an addition to the poem and not written by *Imam Ibn al-Jazari* ﵀. Therefore, it can be said with certainty that the poem has at least 107 lines in total.

تَمَّ شَرْحُ المقدمةِ الجزرية بحمد الله الملك الوهاب و بعونه يوم الاحد ثامن عشر من شهر ذي القعدة سنة 1440 هجرية على يد أَحْوَج عُبَيدِ اللهِ الي مَغفرتِه زين هود الازهري غفر الله له و لوالديه و لإخوانه في الله و لجميع المسلمين . آمين و الحمد لله رب العالمين و صلى الله على سيدنا محمد و على آله و أصحابه و أزواجه و ذُرِّيَّتِه و سلّم تسليما كثيرا دائما أبدا الي يوم الدين . وحسبنا الله و نعم الوكيل و لا حول و لا قوة إلا بالله العليّ العظيم

All praise is for Allah, who allowed this weak servant to complete a brief commentary on the poem *Jazariyyah* on 21 July 2019 at *Darul Itiqaan*, near *Al-Azhar* and the mosque of *Imam Husain*, Cairo, Egypt. May Allah bestow abundant blessings and salutations upon his beloved messenger Muhammad ﷺ .

May Allah forgive our sins and give us the *Tawfiq* to live and die with *Iman*. *Amin*

رَبَّنَآ أَتۡمِمۡ لَنَا نُورَنَا وَٱغۡفِرۡ لَنَآۖ إِنَّكَ عَلَىٰ كُلِّ شَيۡءٖ قَدِيرٞ

TEST

Makharij and *Sifaat*

1. Fill in the Tables below by writing the *Makhraj*, *Sifaat* and the line from the poem, which mentions the *Makhraj*:

***Qaf* (ق)**	
Makhraj:	Sifaat: 1. 2. 3. 4. 5. 6.
Line from the Poem, which mentions the *Makhraj*:	

***Dhad* (ض)**	
Makhraj:	Sifaat: 1. 2. 3. 4. 5. 6.
Line from the Poem, which mentions the *Makhraj*:	

2. Why are the qualities of *Jahr* and *Shiddah* important in the letters *Jeem* and *Ba*?

____

____

____

____

3. Write the two causes that can make the letter *Ra* empty mouth, including the two conditions for the second cause:

First: ___________________________________

Second: _________________________________

Condition 1: ______________________________

____

Condition 2: ______________________________

____

4. Write the two lines from the poem, which mention when the letter *Ra* is read with an empty mouth:

____

____

5. Why is there a dispute in the word فِرْقٍ ?

____

____

____

6. Write out the levels of *Isti'la*:
   a) ____
   b) ____
   c) ____
   d) ____
   e) ____

7. What is the difference between the complete *Idgham* (الادغام التام) and the partial *Idgham* (الادغام الناقص)?

____

____

____

____

8. What is the difference between the letter *Dhad* (ض) and the letter *Zha* (ظ)?

   Makhraj:

   ____

   ____

   ____

   Sifaat:

   ____

   ____

   ____

   Writing:

   ____

   ____

   ____

9. What is the rule of *Ikhfa Shafawiy* and which is it mentioned in?

10. What is *al-Waqt at-Taam*?

11. In which two verses are the words بِئْسَ مَا written jointly?

12. In which verse is there a difference concerning بِئْسَ مَا?

13. In which verse is the word شَجَرَت written with a long *Ta*?